M·99

W/D

Refresher in Basic Mathematics
— 3rd Edition

Professor R. N. ROWE B.Sc, M.Sc, F.I.M.A., C.Math., C.Stat.

Dean, South Bank Business School
South Bank University

THOMSON
™

Australia • Canada • Mexico • Singapore • Spain • United Kingdom • United States

Refresher in Basic Mathematics

Copyright © Nick Rowe 2002

The Thomson logo is a registered trademark used herein under licence.

For more information, contact Thomson Learning, High Holborn House, 50-51 Bedford Row, London WC1R 4LR or visit us on the World Wide Web at:
http://www.thomsonlearning.co.uk

British Library Cataloguing-in-Publication Data
A catalogue record for this book is available from the British Library

ISBN-13: 978-0-8264-5829-7
ISBN-10: 0-8264-5829-7

Third edition first published 2002 by Continuum
Reprinted 2005 by Thomson Learning

Printed in the UK by TJ International, Padstow Cornwall

Acknowledgements

I would like to thank my academic colleagues at South Bank University, especially Les Norman and Pam Dobson. I would also like to thank Geoff Swimer and Diana Bedward, and Derek Penney for his editorial advice with the text. I am indebted to Robin Stenham, Harry Chard, Vernon Parker and colleagues, and to the many students, staff and readers who have commented on the earlier editions of this book. Finally I would like to thank my wife, Celine, for her helpful suggestions and patience.

PREFACE TO THE THIRD EDITION

The third edition of this book builds upon the two earlier editions and takes into account the many suggestions and comments received from students, staff and readers.

This new edition also has an expanded section on the use of calculators. It includes worked examples to illustrate how best to perform calculations and identifies potential pitfalls and common mistakes.

NEED

This book is designed as a 'Self-Help' text which allows students to study and refresh their understanding of Basic Mathematics at their own pace. The first edition of the book resulted from a project, lasting several years, aimed at helping to alleviate the difficulties faced by students entering courses in higher (or further) education where a knowledge equivalent to GCSE Mathematics is assumed. There are many such courses in higher (and further) education, very often multi-disciplinary or inter-disciplinary in nature (in such areas as Business Studies, Accountancy, Social Sciences, Education, Hospital Administration, as well as a whole range of Science courses, etc.), which involve the study of subjects such as Quantitative Methods, Statistics, Mathematics, etc. These courses build upon basic mathematical concepts, and it is clear, from experience, that very many students encounter difficulties at an early stage due to their lengthy absence from studying Mathematics, or even because the basic concepts were not originally understood. This book was written to help meet the needs of such students.

APPROACH

The units should normally be studied in sequence as each unit assumes knowledge of the preceding units. Each unit consists of an introduction to the topic in question, together with a series of graded worked examples (the examples generally becoming progressively more difficult). The worked examples are usually followed by a set of similar exercises in which the student can develop his/her understanding of the concepts and skills displayed in the worked examples. Towards the end of each unit there is a set of 'General Exercises' which tests the student's knowledge of all the material covered throughout that unit. After completing the ten units, the student can assess his/her progress by taking the 'Achievement Test'. Answers are provided at the end of each unit and also at the end of the Achievement Test (a marking scheme and a performance guide are also provided for the Achievement Test).

The 'Tutors Section', which includes extra exercises and an additional Achievement Test for which answers are not provided, will allow tutors to use the exercises/test for homework or assessment purposes.

Professor R. N. Rowe
Dean, South Bank Business School
South Bank University
Borough Road
London SE1 0AA

Telephone 020 7815 8281

CONTENTS

v

1. FRACTIONS

INTRODUCTION

A fraction is a number which can represent part of a whole. For example, consider the following square which is divided into four equal parts (i.e. each part has an equal area).

Fig.1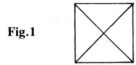

Each part represents one quarter (i.e. ¼)
If we now separate one of the parts in this diagram as follows,

Fig. 2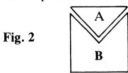

Then the area A represents one quarter (i.e. ¼) of the square, and the area B represents three quarters (i.e. ¾) of the square.

A fraction may also represent a division, e.g. 3 ÷ 4 (= ¾) where 3 is said to be the numerator and 4 the denominator.

A fraction such as ⁴/₆ is said to be equivalent to ²/₃ because if we divide the number 2 into both the numerator and the denominator of ⁴/₆, then it reduces to ²/₃. A fraction such as ²/₃ is said to be in its simplest form because it cannot be reduced any further (i.e. the only number which can be divided into both its numerator and denominator is the number 1).

Fig.3.  **Fig. 4.**

The shaded area in Fig. 3. represents ⁴/₆ of the area of the circle and the shaded area in Fig. 4. represents ²/₃ of the area of the circle

It can be seen from these diagrams that ⁴/₆ = ²/₃

As well as having values less than 1, a fraction may have a value greater than 1, e.g. ⁵/₄, which equals 1 ¼ (see example 2).

Examples of these concepts, as well as the addition, subtraction, multiplication and division of fractions are given below.

EXAMPLE 1

Express ³⁵/₄₀ in its simplest form.

1

Now both the numerator and the denominator can be divided by the number 5. When we perform this operation we obtain

$^7/_8$

This is the simplest form of $^{35}/_{40}$. (Because the numerator and denominator of $^7/_8$ cannot be divided by any number other than 1).

EXERCISES Questions similar to example 1.

Express the following fractions in their simplest form:

i) $^4/_8$
ii) $^{15}/_{25}$
iii) $^{48}/_{64}$
iv) $^{40}/_{56}$
v) $^{121}/_{132}$

EXAMPLE 2

Complete the following: i) $2\,^5/_8 = \,^?/_8$
    ii) $^{20}/_7 = 2\,^?/_7$

i)   We start with $2\,^5/_8$:

We first multiply the whole number part by the denominator of the fraction
(i.e. $2 \times 8 = 16$) and then add the numerator part of the fraction
(i.e. $16 + 5 = 21$)

This total divided by the denominator of the fraction provides our answer.

That is

$$2\,^5/_8 = \,^{21}/_8$$

ii)   We start with $^{20}/_7$;

If we divide 7 into 20 we obtain the answer 2 with a remainder of 6.

We can therefore write

$$^{20}/_7 = 2\,^6/_7$$

(i.e. the remainder divided by the denominator of the original fraction preceded by the whole number part).

EXERCISES   Questions similar to example 2.

Complete the following:

i) $3\,^1/_4 = \,^?/_4$
ii) $5\,^3/_7 = \,^?/_7$
iii) $12\,^{10}/_{11} = \,^?/_{11}$
iv) $^{61}/_8 = 7\,^?/_8$
v) $^{144}/_5 = 28\,^?/_5$

EXAMPLE 3

Evaluate ¾ + ⅛

Expressing ¾ + ⅛ over a common denominator we obtain

$$\frac{3}{4} + \frac{1}{8} = \frac{6+1}{8} = \frac{7}{8}$$

Hence our answer is ⅞

EXAMPLE 4

Evaluate 1 ⁵/₁₂ − ⅜

$$1\,^5/_{12} - \,^3/_8 = \frac{17}{12} - \frac{3}{8} = \frac{34-9}{24} = \frac{25}{24}$$

$$= 1\,^1/_{24}$$

EXAMPLE 5

i)   Evaluate ³/₅ × ⅞
ii) Evaluate ¾ × ²/₉

i)   We have ³/₅ × ⅞

Multiplying the numerators together, and the denominators together, we obtain

$$\frac{3}{5} \times \frac{7}{8} = \frac{3 \times 7}{5 \times 8} = \frac{21}{40}$$

ii) To evaluate ¾ × ²/₉

We can first cancel out, as follows:

$$\frac{\cancel{3}^1}{\cancel{4}_2} \times \frac{\cancel{2}^1}{\cancel{9}_3} = \frac{1}{2} \times \frac{1}{3}$$

Now multiplying the numerators together, and the denominators together, we obtain

$$\frac{1}{2} \times \frac{1}{3} = \frac{1 \times 1}{2 \times 3} = \frac{1}{6}$$

That is $\dfrac{3}{4} \times \dfrac{2}{9} = \dfrac{1}{6}$

Alternatively, without cancelling out, we obtain

$$\frac{3}{4} \times \frac{2}{9} = \frac{3 \times 2}{4 \times 9} = \frac{6}{36} = \frac{1}{6}$$

EXAMPLE 6

Evaluate ²/₃ ÷ 2 ½

Now ⅔ ÷ 2 ½ = ⅔ ÷ ⁵/₂

3

Inverting the divisor and changing the division sign to a multiplication sign we obtain

$$\frac{2}{3} \div \frac{5}{2} = \frac{2}{3} \times \frac{2}{5} = \frac{2 \times 2}{3 \times 5} = \frac{4}{15}$$

EXERCISES   Questions similar to examples 3, 4, 5 and 6.

Evaluate the following:

i) $4/5 + 1/10$
ii) $2\,3/4 + 3/5$
iii) $2\,1/3 - 3/4$
iv) $7\,3/4 - 2\,5/8$
v) $1\,1/2 + 1/6 - 2/3$
vi) $4\,1/2 \times 1/2$
vii) $3/4 \times 2/3$
viii) $4/7 \div 1/4$
ix) $2\,3/4 \div 1\,1/5$
x) $6/11 \div 3\,2/7$

EXAMPLE 7

Evaluate

$$\frac{(2\,\tfrac{1}{2} + 4\,\tfrac{3}{5})}{(1\,\tfrac{1}{6} \times 2\,\tfrac{1}{4})}$$

Let us first look at the numerator of this expression. We have:

$$2\,\tfrac{1}{2} + 4\,\tfrac{3}{5} = \frac{5}{2} + \frac{23}{5} = \frac{25 + 46}{10} = \frac{71}{10} = 7\,\tfrac{1}{10}$$

Similarly, we now look at the denominator and we have:

$$1\,\tfrac{1}{6} \times 2\,\tfrac{1}{4} = \frac{7}{6} \times \frac{9}{4} = \frac{63}{24} = 2\,\tfrac{15}{24} = 2\,\tfrac{5}{8}$$

The original expression now becomes:

$$\frac{(2\,\tfrac{1}{2} + 4\,\tfrac{3}{5})}{(1\,\tfrac{1}{6} \times 2\,\tfrac{1}{4})} = \frac{7\,\tfrac{1}{10}}{2\,\tfrac{5}{8}} = 7\,\tfrac{1}{10} \div 2\,\tfrac{5}{8}$$

$$= \frac{71}{10} \div \frac{21}{8} = \frac{71}{10} \times \frac{8}{21}$$

Cancelling out, as follows, we now have:

$$\frac{71}{\cancel{10}_5} \times \frac{\cancel{8}^4}{21} = \frac{284}{105}$$

$$= 2\,\tfrac{74}{105}$$

GENERAL EXERCISES

Evaluate the following:

i) $5/12 + 7/18$
ii) $\frac{3}{4} + \frac{2}{3}$
iii) $1\frac{3}{8} + 2\frac{1}{6}$
iv) $5/7 - \frac{1}{2}$
v) $7/10 - 1\frac{1}{4}$
vi) $3\frac{3}{8} - 7/16$
vii) $2/7 \times 3/5$
viii) $7/9 \times \frac{3}{4}$
ix) $6 \times 5\frac{3}{8}$
x) $2\frac{1}{4} \times 12$
xi) $6/7 \div \frac{1}{3}$
xii) $2\frac{7}{8} \div 6/7$
xiii) $\frac{1}{4} \div \frac{1}{3}$
xiv) $6/7 \div 3$
xv) $2\frac{7}{8} \div 6$
xvi) $2/3 \div 2/5$
xvii) $1\frac{3}{4} \div 4\frac{1}{2}$
xviii) $4/5 \times 2/7 \times 1\frac{1}{4}$
xix) $(\frac{3}{4} - \frac{1}{3}) \times 2/5$
xx) $(1\frac{3}{4} \times 1\frac{3}{4}) \div 1\frac{1}{4}$
xxi) $\dfrac{(1\frac{1}{8} - \frac{1}{4})}{(1\frac{1}{8} + \frac{1}{4})}$

xxii) $\dfrac{(8\frac{1}{4} \times 1\frac{1}{2})}{(4\frac{1}{2} + 4\frac{1}{4})}$

xxiii) $\dfrac{(3 + 1\frac{3}{4} - 2\frac{1}{3})}{(2/5 \times 1\frac{3}{4})}$

Write the following fractions in order of magnitude, with the greatest one first:

xxiv) $5/8$, $3/5$, $13/20$
xxv) $4/15$, $5/12$, $2/5$, $\frac{1}{3}$

UNIT 1 – FRACTIONS
SOLUTIONS TO EXERCISES

1. Questions similar to example 1.

    i) $\frac{1}{2}$
    ii) $3/5$
    iii) $\frac{3}{4}$
    iv) $5/7$
    v) $11/12$

2. Questions similar to example 2.

   i) $13/4$
   ii) $38/7$
   iii) $142/11$
   vi) $7 5/8$
   v) $28 4/5$

3. Questions similar to example 3, 4, 5 and 6.

   i) $9/10$
   ii) $3 7/20$
   iii) $1 7/12$
   iv) $5 1/8$
   v) 1
   vi) $2 1/4$
   vii) $1/2$
   viii) $2 2/7$
   ix) $2 7/24$
   x) $42/253$

4. General Exercises

   i) $29/36$
   ii) $1 5/12$
   iii) $3 13/24$
   iv) $3/14$
   v) $-11/20$
   vi) $2 15/16$
   vii) $6/35$
   viii) $7/12$
   ix) $32 1/4$
   x) 27
   xi) $2 4/7$
   xii) $3 17/48$
   xiii) $3/4$
   xiv) $2/7$
   xv) $23/48$
   xvi) $1 2/3$
   xvii) $7/18$
   xviii) $2/7$
   xix) $1/6$
   xx) $2 9/20$
   xxi) $7/11$
   xxii) $1 29/70$
   xxiii) $3 19/42$
   xxiv) $13/20, 5/8, 3/5$
   xxv) $5/12, 2/5, 1/3, 4/15$

2. DECIMALS

INTRODUCTION

Decimal notation can be considered as an alternative way of expressing a fraction.

e.g.

$7/10 = 0.7$ $17/10 = 1\,7/10 = 1.7$

$69/100 = 0.69$ $269/100 = 2\,69/100 = 2.69$

The dot is referred to as a 'decimal point'. Digits to the right of the decimal point denote the numbers of tenths, hundreds, thousandths, etc. respectively.

e.g.

$0.4 = 4/10$

$0.04 = 4/100$

$0.004 = 4/1000$

$0.056 = 56/1000$

Expressing the fraction $\frac{1}{3}$ as a decimal we have

$\frac{1}{3} = 0.333.....$ (see example 2)

this is called a recurring decimal and is denoted by $0.\dot{3}$

The multiplication or division of a decimal by a power of 10 can be carried out by an appropriate shift of the decimal point to the right (in multiplication) or to the left (in division).

e.g.

$3.461 \times 100 = 346.1$

$0.00372 \times 1000 = 3.72$

$227.46 \div 10 = 22.746$

$3.57 \div 100 = 0.0357$

N.B. In the above examples, the number of places the decimal point is shifted equals the number of zeros in the multiplier or the divisor.

The method of transforming decimals into fractions, and fractions into decimals, together with the basic decimal operations, are illustrated in the following examples.

EXAMPLE 1

Transform the following decimals into fractions:

i)   0.3

ii)   3.375

iii)   0.003

i)   Transform 0.3 into a fraction

$$0.3 = 3/10$$

(i.e. the first number after the decimal point denotes the number of tenths)

ii)   Transform 3.375 into a fraction

$$3.375 = 3\ ^{375}/_{1000}$$

Note that the number of numbers after the decimal point equals the number of zeros below the line in the fraction.

The fraction $3\ ^{375}/_{1000}$ can be simplified by dividing above and below the line by 125. Thus we have:

$$3.375 = 3\ ^{375}/_{1000} = \mathbf{3\ ^3/_8}$$

iii)   Transform 0.003 into a fraction.

$$0.003 = ^3/_{1000}$$

Note, again, that the number of numbers after the decimal point equals the number of zeros below the line in the fraction.

EXERCISES   Questions similar to example 1.

Transform the following decimals into fractions:

i)   0.5
ii)   0.387
iii)   0.00205
iv)   3.007401
v)   – 2.300

EXAMPLE 2

Transform the following fractions into decimals:

i) $^1/_5$
ii) $2\ ^3/_4$
iii) $^2/_3$

i)   Transform $^1/_5$ into a decimal

We divide the denominator into the numerator

i.e

$$5 \overline{)1.0} \quad \begin{array}{c} 0.2 \end{array}$$

We introduce the decimal point as soon as it becomes necessary to add a zero after the numerator in order to continue the division.

Thus, we have $^1/_5 = \mathbf{0.2}$

ii)   Transform $2\ ^3/_4$ into a decimal

We need only consider the $^3/_4$ (the whole number part remains the same).

Again, we divide the denominator into the numerator.

i.e.

$$
\begin{array}{r}
0.75 \\
4\,\overline{)3.00} \\
2\,8 \\
\hline
20 \\
20 \\
\hline
0
\end{array}
$$

Thus, we have

$$2\,\tfrac{3}{4} \;=\; \mathbf{2.75}$$

iii)   Transform ⅔ into a decimal.

Dividing the denominator into the numerator we have

$$
\begin{array}{r}
0.666\ldots \\
3\,\overline{)2.000}
\end{array}
$$

Thus we have $^2/_3$ = **0.666....** (a recurring decimal denoted by **0.6̇**)

EXERCISES   Questions similar to example 2.

Transform the following fractions into decimals:

i) $^7/_{10}$
ii) $2\,^{15}/_{16}$
iii) $-\,3\,^9/_{40}$
iv) $-\,^5/_{32}$
v) $^7/_{15}$

EXAMPLE 3

Add 3.81 + 0.002 + 21.4

The first step is to line up these numbers, one beneath the other, with the decimal points forming a vertical line. We then add in the usual way.

$$
\begin{array}{r}
3.81 \\
0.002 \\
21.4 \\
\hline
25.212
\end{array}
$$

Our answer is **25.212**

EXAMPLE 4

Subtract 2.1476 from 4.002
(i.e. 4.002 − 2.1476)

First we line up these numbers with the decimal points underneath each other.

9

We now have

$$
\begin{array}{r}
4.0020 \\
-\ 2.1476 \\
\hline
1.8544
\end{array}
$$

Thus, after subtracting in the usual way, our answer is **1.8544**

N.B. 4.002 and 4.0020 are exactly the same. An extra zero on the extreme right of a decimal does not affect it.

EXERCISES   Questions similar to examples 3 and 4.

Evaluate the following:
i) $0.47\ +\ 3.846\ +\ 2.00360$
ii) $2.51\ -\ 0.00037$
iii) $26.57\ +\ 14.01\ +\ 15$
iv) $12.03\ -\ 1.42$
v) $2.31\ -\ 4.06\ +\ 5.7$

EXAMPLE 5

Multiply 12.371 by 2.1

We first multiply these numbers together ignoring the decimal points and do not concern ourselves with the position of the decimal point in our answer until after the multiplication has been performed. That is

$$
\begin{array}{r}
12371 \\
\times\ 21 \\
\hline
247420 \\
12371 \\
\hline
259791
\end{array}
$$

Now in our original problem there were, in both the numbers, a total of four digits on the right hand side of the decimal points. Therefore, to obtain our final answer, we ensure that there are four digits to the right of the decimal point in the solution to the multiplication already performed.

Thus our answer is **25.9791**

EXERCISES   Questions similar to example 5.

Evaluate the following:
i) $4.2\ \times\ 3$
ii) $5.6\ \times\ 2.1$
iii) $2.004\ \times\ 3.2$
iv) $4.56\ \times\ 0.0003$
v) $2.41\ \times\ 5.60$

EXAMPLE 6

Divide 0.35 by 2.5

The first step is to ensure that the divisor (i.e. 2.5) is a whole number, so we thus multiply both numbers in the question by an appropriate power of 10.

That is

$$0.35 \div 2.5 = 3.5 \div 25$$

(i.e. we move the decimal point one place to the right in both numbers)

Now dividing in the usual way we have

```
        0.14
  25 ) 3.50
        2 5
        1 00
        1 00
           0
```

Thus our answer is **0.14**

EXERCISES   Questions similar to example 6.

Evaluate the following:

i) $4.6 \div 2$
ii) $2.306 \div 0.2$
iii) $1.73664 \div 0.324$
iv) $2.35124 \div 0.86$
v) $0.01081 \div 2.35$

EXAMPLE 7

Evaluate

$$\frac{(1.2 \times 5.1)}{(3.2 - 1.76)}$$

Let us first look at the numerator of this expression. We have:

$1.2 \times 5.1 = 6.12$ (Using the method illustrated in example 5)

Similarly, we now look at the denominator and we have:

$3.2 - 1.76 = 1.44$ (Using the method illustrated in example 4)

The original expression now becomes:

$$\frac{(1.2 \times 5.1)}{(3.2 - 1.76)} = \frac{6.12}{1.44} = 6.12 \div 1.44$$

Now, using the method illustrated in example 6, we have:

$6.12 \div 1.44 = \textbf{4.25}$

GENERAL EXERCISES

i)   Transform $5/9$ into a decimal
ii)   Transform 0.312 into a fraction

Evaluate the following:

iii) $2.413 + 0.165$
iv) $4.073 + 2.86 + 5.4$
v) $3.47 - 0.8$
vi) $4 - 1.003$
vii) 61.457×10
viii) 61.457×100
ix) 36.57×0.003
x) 4.26×7.5
xi) 3.546×9
xii) $24.37 \div 10$
xiii) $24.37 \div 10000$
xiv) $17.36 \div 7$
xv) $49.375 \div 12.5$
xvi) $0.002 \div 0.016$
xvii) $2.316 + 47.2 + 1 - 16.03$
xviii) 17×4.05
xix) $12 \div 0.0024$
xx) $- 3.45 \div 1.5$
xxi) $\dfrac{(2.8 - 1.046 + 3)}{0.16}$
xxii) $(4.3 - 12.71) \times 0.02$

UNIT 2 – DECIMALS
SOLUTIONS TO EXERCISES

1. Questions similar to example 1.
    i) $\frac{1}{2}$
    ii) $387/1000$
    iii) $205/100000 = 41/20000$
    iv) $3\,7401/1000000$
    v) $- 2\,3/10$

2. Questions similar to example 2.
    i) 0.7
    ii) 2.9375
    iii) $- 3.225$
    vi) $- 0.15625$
    v) $0.4\dot{6}$

3. Questions similar to example 3 and 4.
    i)   6.3196
    ii)   2.50963
    iii)   55.58
    iv)   10.61
    v)   3.95

4. Questions similar to example 5.
    i)   12.6
    ii)   11.76
    iii)   6.4128
    iv)   0.001368
    v)   13.496

5. Questions similar to example 6.
    i)   2.3
    ii)   11.53
    iii)   5.36
    iv)   2.734
    v)   0.0046

6. General Exercises
    i) $0.\dot{5}$
    ii) $^{39}/_{125}$
    iii)   2.578
    iv)   12.333
    v)   2.67
    vi)   2.997
    vii)   614.57
    viii)   6145.7
    ix)   0.10971
    x)   31.95
    xi)   31.914
    xii)   2.437
    xiii)   0.002437
    xiv)   2.48
    xv)   3.95
    xvi)   0.125
    xvii)   34.486
    xviii) 68.85
    xix)   5000
    xx)   − 2.3
    xxi)   29.7125
    xxii)   − 0.1682

3. PERCENTAGES

INTRODUCTION

The expression 'percent' (Latin 'per centum') means for every hundred. Twenty per cent means 20 out of every hundred and is equivalent to $^{20}/_{100}$ (or $^{1}/_{5}$). Twenty per cent is written, using the symbol % to represent percent, as 20%.

A fraction which has the denominator equal to 100 may be expressed as a percentage by simply writing down the numerator.

e.g. $^{56}/_{100}$ may be written as 56%

$^{2}/_{100}$ may be written as 2%

More generally, to convert a fraction to a percentage the fraction must be multiplied by 100.

e.g.   To express $^{2}/_{5}$ as a percentage we have

$$^{2}/_{5} \times 100 = {}^{200}/_{5} = 40$$

so that we can now say $^{2}/_{5}$ is equivalent to 40%

To convert a decimal to a percentage simply multiply the decimal by 100 (i.e. move the decimal point two places to the right)

e.g.   0.025 is equivalent to 2.5%

To calculate a certain percentage of a given amount we consider the percentage as a decimal (or a fraction) and then multiply it by the amount in question. That is, to calculate 10% of 80, say, we calculate ten hundredths of 80.

e.g. 10% of $80 = {}^{10}/_{100} \times 80 = 8$

or

$= 0.1 \times 80 = 8$

EXAMPLE 1

Express the following fractions as percentages:

i) $^{3}/_{25}$
ii) $^{1}/_{8}$

i)   If we multiply $^{3}/_{25}$ by 100 we obtain the desired result.

i.e.

$$\frac{3}{25} \times \frac{100}{1} = 12$$

therefore $^{3}/_{25}$ is equivalent to **12%**

14

ii)   To convert ⅛ to a percentage we must again multiply by 100. We thus obtain

$$\frac{1}{8} \times \frac{100}{1} = \frac{100}{8} = 12\,½$$

therefore ⅛ is equivalent to **12 ½ %**

EXERCISES   Questions similar to example 1.
Express the following fractions as percentages:

   i)   ¹/₅
   ii) ¾
   iii) ²⁹³/₄₀₀

EXAMPLE 2
Express the following percentages as fractions:

   i)   15%
   ii) 18 ½%

i)   To express 15% as a fraction we simply put 15 over the denominator of 100.   15% is thus equivalent to ¹⁵/₁₀₀ which, if we divide above and below the line by 5, reduces to ³/₂₀.
Therefore 15% is equivalent to **³/₂₀**

ii) 18 ½% is equivalent to

$$\frac{18\,½}{100}$$

In order to get rid of the '½' in the numerator we can multiply above and below the line by 2, and we thus obtain ³⁷/₂₀₀.
Therefore 18 ½% is equivalent to **³⁷/₂₀₀**

EXERCISES   Questions similar to example 2.
Express the following percentages as fractions:

   i)   35%
   ii) 6%
   iii) 15 ¼%

EXAMPLE 3
Express the following decimals as percentages:

   i)   0.3
   ii) 0.075

i)   To convert 0.3 to a percentage we multiply 0.3 by 100. We thus obtain 0.3 × 100 = 30
        Therefore 0.3 is equivalent to **30%**

ii)   If we multiply 0.075 by 100 we obtain 7.5

Therefore 0.075 is equivalent to **7.5% or 7 ½%**

EXERCISES   Questions similar to example 3.

Express the following decimals as percentages:
  i)   0.39
  ii)   0.065
  iii)   0.7004

EXAMPLE 4

Express the following percentages as decimals:
  i)   85%
  ii)   4%

i)   To convert 85% to a decimal we must divide 85 by 100.

Thus 85% is equivalent to the decimal **0.85**

ii)   To convert 4% to a decimal we divide 4 by 100, and hence obtain 0.04.

Therefore 4% is equivalent to the decimal **0.04**

EXERCISES   Questions similar to example 4.

Express the following percentages as decimals:
  i)   17%
  ii)   2%
  iii)   9 ⅝%

EXAMPLE 5
  i)   Calculate 12% of 250
  ii)   Calculate 62 ¼% of 80

i)   To calculate 12% of 250 we first express 12% as a decimal and then multiply it by 250.

Thus we have

$$0.12 \times 250 = 30$$

Therefore 12% of 250 equals **30.**

ii)   62 ¼% can be expressed, in decimal form, as 0.6225.

Therefore 62 ¼% of 80 is given by

$$0.6225 \times 80 = \mathbf{49.8}$$

EXERCISES   Questions similar to example 5.
  i)   Calculate 8% of 150
  ii)   Calculate 57% of 63
  iii)   Calculate 15 ⅝% of 400

EXAMPLE 6

   i)   Increase 250 by 5%

   ii)   Increase 380 by 12%

   iii)   Decrease 450 by 7½%

i)   To increase 250 by 5% we can calculate 5% of 250 and add this amount to 250.

    i.e.

$$250 + 250(0.05)$$
$$= 250 + 12.5$$
$$= \mathbf{262.5}$$

    Alternatively, we can multiply 250 by $(1 + 0.05)$

    i.e.

$$250(1 + 0.05)$$
$$= 250(1.05)$$
$$= \mathbf{262.5}$$

ii)   To increase 380 by 12% we can multiply 380 by $(1 + 0.12)$

    i.e.

$$380(1 + 0.12)$$
$$= 380(1.12)$$
$$= \mathbf{425.6}$$

iii) To decrease 450 by 7 ½% we can multiply 450 by $(1 - 0.075)$

    i.e.

$$450(1 - 0.075)$$
$$= 450(0.925)$$
$$= \mathbf{416.25}$$

EXERCISES   Questions similar to example 6.

   i)   Increase 25 by 10%

   ii)   Increase 136 by 60%

   iii)   Increase 58 by 7¼%

   iv)   Decrease 300 by 15%

   v)   Decrease 270 by 3⅕%

GENERAL EXERCISES

   i)   Express ²/₅ as a percentage

   ii)   Express ⁷/₁₀ as a percentage

   iii)   Express 0.31 as a percentage

   iv)   Express 0.07125 as a percentage

   v)   Express 0.8346875 as a percentage

   vi)   Express ⁵/₆₄ as a percentage

   vii)   Express ¹³/₁₆ as a percentage

   viii) Express 13% as a fraction

   ix)   Express 56% as a decimal

x)   Express 33 ¼% as a fraction
xi)   Express 89 ³/₂₅% as a decimal
xii)   Calculate 17% of 1000
xiii)   Calculate 53% of 37
xiv)   Calculate 18 ¾% of 546
xv)   Calculate 5 ¹/₆₄% of 310
xvi)   Increase 400 by 12%
xvii)   Increase 26 by 91 ½%
xviii) Increase 746 by 4 ¹/₃₂%
xix)   Decrease 700 by 53%
xx)   Decrease 10 by 3 ¾%

UNIT 3 – PERCENTAGES
SOLUTIONS TO EXERCISES

1. Questions similar to example 1.
    i)   20%
    ii)   75%
    iii)   73 ¼% = 73.25%

2. Questions similar to example 2.
    i)   ⁷/₂₀
    ii)   ³/₅₀
    iii)   ⁶¹/₄₀₀

3. Questions similar to example 3.
    i)   39%
    ii)   6 ½% = 6.5%
    iii)   70 ¹/₂₅% = 70.04%

4. Questions similar to example 4.
    i)   0.17
    ii)   0.02
    iii)   0.09625

5. Questions similar to example 5.
    i)   12
    ii)   35.91
    iii)   62.5

6. Questions similar to example 6.
    i)   27.5
    ii)   217.6
    iii)   62.205
    iv)   255
    v)   261.36

7. General Exercises

i)	40%
ii)	70%
iii)	31%
iv)	7 $\frac{1}{8}$% = 7.125%
v)	83 $^{15}/_{32}$% = 83.46875%
vi)	7 $^{13}/_{16}$% = 7.8125%
vii)	81 $\frac{1}{4}$% = 81.25%
viii)	$^{13}/_{100}$
ix)	0.56
x)	$^{133}/_{400}$
xi)	0.8912
xii)	170
xiii)	19.61
xiv)	102.375
xv)	15.548437
xvi)	448
xvii)	49.79
xviii)	776.073125
xix)	329
xx)	9.625

4. ELEMENTARY ALGEBRA

INTRODUCTION

Consider the case where one number is multiplied by another or divided into another. If the two numbers have the same sign then the answer will be a positive number. If, however, the two numbers have different signs then the answer will be a negative number *(N.B. When no sign precedes a number it is taken to be positive)*

e.g.
$$(+5) \times (+3) = +15$$
$$(-5) \times (-3) = +15$$
$$(+2) \times (-4) = -8$$
$$(-2) \times (+4) = -8$$
$$(+8) \div (+2) = +4$$
$$(-8) \div (-2) = +4$$
$$(-6) \div (+3) = -2$$
$$(+6) \div (-3) = -2$$

A VARIABLE is the name given to a characteristic or quantity that varies (i.e. it can take a range of values). In mathematics it is often necessary to study 'variables' such as 'Time', 'Weight', 'Length', 'Amount' etc. Usually variables are represented by letters of the alphabet (e.g. X, Y). For example, X may represent any number in the set of natural numbers 1, 2, 3,...

A variable may be CONTINUOUS or DISCRETE. A continuous variable is one which can assume any numerical value within a specified range, e.g. 'the weight of individual students in a class'. A discrete variable is one which can only take certain numerical values (for example, integers) within a specified range e.g. 'the number of children per family on a housing estate'.

A CONSTANT is a characteristic or quantity that does not vary (i.e. it always has the same value).

e.g. π is a constant
       3 is a constant
       -7 is a constant.

INEQUALITIES are often used to express the relationship between variables and/or constants. They are defined as follows:

If a and b are two numbers then

$a < b$ means a is less than b
$a \leqslant b$ means a is less than or equal to b
$a > b$ means a is greater than b
$a \geqslant b$ means a is greater than or equal to b.

For example, if X represents the number of days in a year in which it rains, then we can say

$$0 \leqslant X \leqslant 365 \text{ (or 366 if a leap year)}$$

ALGEBRAIC OPERATIONS

Using algebra we may add positive and/or negative quantities. For example the sum of $+ m$ and $- n$ can be written as $+ m - n$, or simply $m - n$ (the $+$ sign being assumed for m when no sign is written). Thus if, for example, $m = 15$ and $n = 3$ then $m - n = 15 - 3 = 12$.

Algebraic expressions such as $3x$, ab, $7xy$ all represent products.

$3x = 3$ multiplied by x
$ab = a$ multiplied by b
$7xy = 7$ multiplied by x multiplied by y

In the expression $3x$, 3 is referred to as the *coefficient* of x. Similarly, in the expression $7xy$, 7 is referred to as the coefficient of xy. (In the expression ab, the coefficient of ab is 1).

(N.B. As in arithmetic, the product $ab = ba$)

If a quantity is multiplied by itself several times, then the product can be expressed using a *power* (or *index*).

For example
$$4 \times 4 \times 4 = 4^3$$

Here we have calculated 4 to the third power – the number '3' can be referred to as the power or index.

Another example is
$$a \times a \times a \times a \times a = a^5$$

Here we have calculated 'a' to the fifth power – the number '5' can be referred to as the power or index.

Similarly,
$$a \times a \times b \times b \times b = a^2 b^3$$

(Powers are dealt with in more detail in unit 5).

The basic operations of algebra are the same as those of arithmetic. To add together 'like terms' we simply add the coefficients. If, however, 'unlike terms' are involved then we must keep these 'unlike terms' separate. This is illustrated in the following example.

EXAMPLE 1

i) $5x + 2x = 7x$
ii) $3x^3 + 5x^3 = 8x^3$
iii) $4ab^2 - 2ab^2 + 7ab^2 = 9ab^2$

The following contain 'unlike terms'.

iv) $3x^3 - 4a^2 + 2x^3 = 5x^3 - 4a^2$
v) $2x + 2y + 3x = 5x + 2y$
vi) $6ab + 2x^2 - ab + x = 5ab + 2x^2 + x$

21

EXERCISES   Questions similar to example 1.

Simplify the following (by combining like terms):

i) $7x + 12x - 3x$
ii) $14f + 3f - 5f + f$
iii) $\frac{1}{5} ab - 4ab + 9 \frac{4}{5} ab$
iv) $y/5 - 4y/15$
v) $12x + 8y - 3x$

Evaluate the following for $x = 2$ and $y = 3$:

vi) $7x + 2y$
vii) $4y - 7x + 8$
viii) $2x/5 + 3y/10$

In an algebraic expression involving multiplication of terms, a FACTOR is any term that can be multiplied to give the product in question.

EXAMPLE 2

i)   5 is a factor of 15
ii)   3 is a factor of 15
iii) x is a factor of x^4
iv)   4a is a factor of $4ax^5y^2$
v) $3x^4$ is a factor of $3x^4y + 6x^4z^2$

Algebraic expressions often involve symbols of grouping such as brackets. A group of terms within brackets is treated as a single expression. Examples of the use of brackets are given below:

EXAMPLE 3

Consider the terms a, b, x, and y, which represent real numbers.

i)   The term a mulitplied by the sum of $x + y$ can be written as **a(x + y)**.

ii)   The sum of $a + b$ multiplied by the sum of $x + y$ can be written as **(a+b)(x+y)**.

It is sometimes necessary to expand an expression involving brackets. Examples of this are given below.

iii) Expanding $a(x + y)$ we obtain
$$a(x + y) = \mathbf{ax + ay}$$

iv)   Expanding $a(x - y)$ we obtain
$$a(x - y) = \mathbf{ax - ay}$$

v)   Expanding $x(x + y)$ we obtain
$$x(x + y) = \mathbf{x^2 + xy}$$

vi)   Expanding $(a + b)(x + y)$ we obtain
$$(a + b)(x + y) = a(x + y) + b(x + y)$$
$$= \mathbf{ax + ay + bx + by}$$

vii) Expanding $(x + y)^2$ we obtain

$$\begin{aligned}(x + y)^2 &= (x + y)(x + y)\\ &= x(x + y) + y(x + y)\\ &= x^2 + xy + yx + y^2\\ &= \mathbf{x^2 + 2xy + y^2}\end{aligned}$$

viii) Expanding $(x - y)^2$ we obtain

$$\begin{aligned}(x-y)^2 &= (x-y)(x-y)\\ &= x(x-y)-y(x-y)\\ &= x^2-xy-yx + y^2\\ &= \mathbf{x^2-2xy + y^2}\end{aligned}$$

ix) Expanding $(x + y)(x - y)$ we obtain

$$\begin{aligned}(x + y)(x-y) &= x(x-y) + y(x-y)\\ &= x^2-xy + yx-y^2\\ &= \mathbf{x^2-y^2}\end{aligned}$$

EXERCISES   Questions similar to examples 2 and 3.

Find all the factors of the following:

i)   15
ii) x^3
iii)   3ab

Expand the following:

iv) $2(x + y)$
v) $6(2x - y)$
vi) $x(x + 2y)$
vii) $3x(x^2 - y)$
viii) $a(4x - y)$
ix) $y(a - 3y)$
x) $(x + y)(x - y)$
xi) $3(a - b)(a + b)$
xii) $(x - 4y)^2$

It is sometimes necessary to simplify an expression by factorising it (i.e. by introducing brackets). Examples of this are given below:

EXAMPLE 4

i)   Consider the expression $4x^3 + 3x$
       As both terms in this expression contain a common factor, x, we can write the expression as follows:
       $$4x^3 + 3x = x(4x^2 + 3)$$

ii)   Consider the expression $8x^5 - 6x^4 + 4x^3$.
       As the three terms in this expression contain a common factor, $2x^3$, we can write the expression as follows:
       $$8x^5 - 6x^4 + 4x^3 = 2x^3(4x^2 - 3x + 2)$$

EXERCISES   Questions similar to example 4.

Factorise the following:

i) $3x^2 - 4x$
ii) $8a^2b - 2a^2b^2$
iii) $4xz - 4z$
iv) $12a^2bc - 8ab^3c - 4abc$
v) $x^3z^2 - 8x^2z - x^2yz$

EXAMPLE 5

   i)   Factorise
$$\frac{p^3x^2}{q} + \frac{p^2x}{q^2}$$

   ii)   Expand
$$\frac{3}{xy}\left[2x - \frac{y}{10}\right]\left[y - \frac{x}{5}\right]$$

i) $\dfrac{p^3x^2}{q} + \dfrac{p^2x}{q^2}$

   As both terms in this expression contain a common factor

   i.e. $\dfrac{p^2x}{q}$

   We can write the expression as follows:

$$\frac{p^3x^2}{q} + \frac{p^2x}{q^2} = \frac{p^2x}{q}\left(px + \frac{1}{q}\right)$$

ii) $\dfrac{3}{xy}\left[2x - \dfrac{y}{10}\right]\left[y - \dfrac{x}{5}\right]$

   This expression contains three terms multiplied together. Using the methods illustrated in example 3 we first multiply two of the terms together and then multiply this result by the third term to get our answer.

   Let us first multiply the two terms in brackets. Using the method illustrated in example 3 vi) we have:

$$\left[2x - \frac{y}{10}\right]\left[y - \frac{x}{5}\right] = 2x\left[y - \frac{x}{5}\right] - \frac{y}{10}\left[y - \frac{x}{5}\right]$$

$$= 2xy - \frac{2x^2}{5} - \frac{y^2}{10} + \frac{xy}{50}$$

   (Adding the terms in xy we have)

$$= \frac{101\,xy}{50} - \frac{2x^2}{5} - \frac{y^2}{10}$$

24

We must now multiply this result by the third term in our original expression (using the method illustrated in examples 3 iii), iv) and v)). We have

$$\frac{3}{xy}\left[2x - \frac{y}{10}\right]\left[y - \frac{x}{5}\right] = \frac{3}{xy}\left[\frac{101\,xy}{50} - \frac{2x^2}{5} - \frac{y^2}{10}\right]$$

$$= \frac{303\,xy}{50\,xy} - \frac{6x^2}{5xy} - \frac{3y^2}{10xy} = \frac{303}{50} - \frac{6x}{5y} - \frac{3y}{10x}$$

$$= 6\,{}^{3}\!/_{50} - {}^{6x}\!/_{5y} - {}^{3y}\!/_{10x}$$

GENERAL EXERCISES

Simplify the following (by combining like terms):

i) $4ab^2 - 8x + 9ab^2 - x$
ii) $7p + 8q - 3p - 2q$
iii) $18x + 3y - 22x - y$
iv) $3a + 4b - a^2b - 2a - 4b$
v) ${}^{4x}\!/_{5} - {}^{2y}\!/_{3} + {}^{x}\!/_{10} - {}^{y}\!/_{9}$

Expand the following:

vi) $(x-4)(x-3)$
vii) $(2y-1)(1-x)$
viii) $(x^2-3)(4-x)$
ix) $4(2x-3)^2$
x) $(x-1)(x-2)(x-3)$
xi) $(x-2)(y+x-3)$
xii) $4(2x-y)(3y-5x)$
xiii) $(p+q+r)(p+q-r)$
xiv) $(2a-b-3c)^2$

Factorise the following:

xv) $xy^2 + xyz$
xvi) $a^3bc^2 - a^2b^2c - abc$
xvii) $\dfrac{x^3z^2}{y} - \dfrac{x}{y^2}$

Expand the following:

xviii) $\dfrac{2(4y-3)}{3}$

xix) $\dfrac{x(x-2)}{3}$

xx) $\dfrac{4(a^2 + 5ab)}{5}$

xxi) $\dfrac{3x}{4}\left[y - \dfrac{z}{3}\right]$

xxii) $\left[\dfrac{x}{3}+\dfrac{y}{2}\right][x-y]$

xxiii) $\dfrac{1}{5}\left[\dfrac{2x}{3}-1\right]\left[\dfrac{x}{4}+1\right]$

xxiv) $pq\left[\dfrac{4q}{5}-\dfrac{p}{3}\right]$

xxv) $\dfrac{1}{xy}\left[\dfrac{2x}{3}-\dfrac{y}{4}\right]\left[\dfrac{4x}{5}-\dfrac{2z}{7}\right]$

UNIT 4 – ELEMENTARY ALGEBRA
SOLUTIONS TO EXERCISES

1. Questions similar to example 1.
   i) $16x$
   ii) $13f$
   iii) $6ab$
   iv) $-y/15$
   v) $9x + 8y$
   vi) 20
   vii) 6
   viii) $1\,7/10$

2. Questions similar to examples 2 and 3.
   i) $1, 3, 5, 15$
   ii) $1, x, x^2, x^3$
   iii) $1, 3, a, b, 3a, 3b, ab, 3ab$
   iv) $2x + 2y$
   v) $12x - 6y$
   vi) $x^2 + 2xy$
   vii) $3x^3 - 3xy$
   viii) $4ax - ay$
   ix) $ay - 3y^2$
   x) $x^2 - y^2$
   xi) $3a^2 - 3b^2$
   xii) $x^2 - 8xy + 16y^2$

3. Questions similar to example 4.
   i) $x(3x - 4)$
   ii) $2a^2b(4 - b)$
   iii) $4z(x - 1)$
   iv) $4abc(3a - 2b^2 - 1)$
   v) $x^2z(xz - 8 - y)$

4. General Exercises

i) $13ab^2 - 9x$

ii) $4p + 6q$

iii) $2y - 4x$

iv) $a - a^2b$

v) $9x/10 - 7y/9$

vi) $x^2 - 7x + 12$

vii) $x + 2y - 2xy - 1$

viii) $-x^3 + 4x^2 + 3x - 12$

ix) $16x^2 - 48x + 36$

x) $x^3 - 6x^2 + 11x - 6$

xi) $x^2 - 5x - 2y + xy + 6$

xii) $44xy - 40x^2 - 12y^2$

xiii) $p^2 + q^2 - r^2 + 2pq$

xiv) $4a^2 + b^2 + 9c^2 - 4ab - 12ac + 6bc$

xv) $xy(y + z)$

xvi) $abc(a^2c - ab - 1)$

xvii) $\dfrac{x}{y} \left[x^2z^2 - \dfrac{1}{y} \right]$

xviii) $\dfrac{8y}{3} - 2$

xix) $\dfrac{x^2}{3} - \dfrac{2x}{3}$

xx) $\dfrac{4a^2}{5} + 4ab$

xxi) $\dfrac{3xy}{4} - \dfrac{xz}{4}$

xxii) $\dfrac{x^2}{3} + \dfrac{xy}{6} - \dfrac{y^2}{2}$

xxiii) $\dfrac{x^2}{30} + \dfrac{x}{12} - \dfrac{1}{5}$

xxiv) $\dfrac{4pq^2}{5} - \dfrac{p^2q}{3}$

xxv) $\dfrac{8x}{15y} - \dfrac{4z}{21y} + \dfrac{z}{14x} - \dfrac{1}{5}$

5. POWERS

INTRODUCTION

The term a^n, where 'a' and 'n' are numbers, means 'a' multiplied by itself 'n' times.

That is

$$a^n = a \times a \times a \dots\dots n \text{ times}$$

'n' is referred to as the power (or exponent or index)

For example

$$8^3 = 8 \times 8 \times 8 = 512$$
$$5^4 = 5 \times 5 \times 5 \times 5 = 625$$
$$(-4)^2 = (-4) \times (-4) = +16$$

a^1 is usually written as just a. (that is, the 'one' is taken as understood and is not written down).

a^2 is read as 'a to the power of 2' or 'a squared'
a^3 is read as 'a to the power of 3' or 'a cubed'
a^n is read as 'a to the power of n'

Further

$$\left[\frac{a}{b} \right]^n = \frac{a^n}{b^n}$$

For example

$$\left[\frac{3}{5} \right]^2 = \frac{3^2}{5^2} = \frac{9}{25}$$

Any number to the power zero equals 1.

That is

$$a^o = 1$$

The basic rules for the manipulation of powers (indices) are illustrated in the following examples.

a) THE MULTIPLICATION RULE

$$a^m \times a^n = a^{m+n}$$

EXAMPLE 1

Evaluate: (i) $\quad 4^2 \times 4^3$
(ii) $\quad 3^7 \times 3^5$

i) Evaluate $4^2 \times 4^3$

Using the mulitplication rule, we have
$$4^2 \times 4^3 = 4^{2+3} = \mathbf{4^5}$$

This can be illustrated as follows:

$4^2 \times 4^3 = (4 \times 4) \times (4 \times 4 \times 4)$
$= 4 \times 4 \times 4 \times 4 \times 4 = 4^5$

ii) Evaluate $3^7 \times 3^5$

Using the multiplication rule, we have

$3^7 \times 3^5 = 3^{7+5} = \mathbf{3^{12}}$

N.B. This rule does not apply to an example like
$$2^3 \times 4^7$$
as '2' and '4' are different numbers.

EXERCISES   Questions similar to example 1.

Evaluate:

i) $2^3 \times 2^5$
ii) $4^2 \times 4^7$
iii) $(3\,\tfrac{1}{2})^2 \times (3\,\tfrac{1}{2})^5$
iv) $x^4(x^7)$
v) $q^a \times q^b$

b) THE DIVISION RULE

$$a^m \div a^n = a^{m-n}$$

EXAMPLE 2

Evaluate: i) $7^3 \div 7^2$
            ii) $6^8 \div 6^5$

i)   Evaluate $7^3 \div 7^2$

Using the division rule we have

$7^3 \div 7^2 = 7^{3-2} = 7^1 = \mathbf{7}$

This can be illustrated as follows:

$$7^3 \div 7^2 \quad = \quad \frac{7^3}{7^2} \quad = \quad \frac{7 \times 7 \times 7}{7 \times 7}$$

Cancelling out above and below the line we obtain

$$\frac{\cancel{7} \times \cancel{7} \times 7}{\cancel{7} \times \cancel{7}} \quad = \quad 7$$

ii) Evaluate $6^8 \div 6^5$

Using the division rule we have

$6^8 \div 6^5 = 6^{8-5} = \mathbf{6^3}$

EXERCISES   Questions similar to example 2.

Evaluate:
i) $3^7 \div 3^4$
ii) $5^8 \div 5^2$
iii) $(12.75)^5 \div (12.75)^4$
iv) $x^{13} \div x^2$
v) $y^5 \div y$

c) NEGATIVE POWERS

$$a^{-n} = \frac{1}{a^n}$$

EXAMPLE 3

Evaluate: i) 3^{-2}
           ii) $5^3 \div 5^6$

i)   Evaluate 3^{-2}

Using the rule for Negative Powers we have

$$3^{-2} = \frac{1}{3^2} = \frac{1}{9}$$

ii)   Evaluate $5^3 \div 5^6$

Using the Division Rule and then the rule for Negative Powers we have

$$5^3 \div 5^6 = 5^{3-6} = 5^{-3} = \frac{1}{5^3} = \frac{1}{125}$$

We can use this example to illustrate the rule for negative powers as follows:

$$5^3 \div 5^6 = \frac{\cancel{5} \times \cancel{5} \times \cancel{5}}{\cancel{5} \times \cancel{5} \times \cancel{5} \times 5 \times 5 \times 5} = \frac{1}{5^3}$$

Also, using the Division Rule,

$$5^3 \div 5^6 = 5^{-3}$$

Therefore $5^{-3} = \frac{1}{5^3}$

EXERCISES   Questions similar to example 3.

Evaluate:
i) 5^{-2}
ii) 3^{-4}
iii) $2^5 \div 2^7$
iv) $4^8 \div 4^{11}$
v) $x^4 \div x^5$
vi) $p \div p^5$

d) POWER OF POWERS

$$(a^m)^n = a^{mn}$$

EXAMPLE 4

Evaluate: i) $(2^2)^3$
        ii) $(5^4)^2$

i)   Evaluate $(2^2)^3$

Using this rule we have $(2^2)^3 = 2^{2 \times 3} = 2^6 =$ **64**
This can be illustrated as follows:
$$(2^2)^3 \quad = (2 \times 2) \times (2 \times 2) \times (2 \times 2)$$
$$= 2 \times 2 \times 2 \times 2 \times 2 \times 2 = 2^6 = 64$$

ii)   Evaluate $(5^4)^2$

Again using this rule we have
$$(5^4)^2 = 5^{4 \times 2} = 5^8$$

EXERCISES   Questions similar to example 4.
Evaluate:
i) $(3^2)^2$
ii) $(4^3)^3$
iii) $(10^2)^4$
iv) $(x^4)^5$
v) $(z^2)^7$

e) FRACTIONAL POWERS

$$a^{m/n} \quad = \sqrt[n]{a^m} \qquad (\text{i.e. the } n^{th} \text{ root of } a^m)$$
$$= (\sqrt[n]{a})^m$$

In particular $a^{1/n} \quad = \sqrt[n]{a}$

This can be illustrated by using the Multiplication Rule to verify, for example, that
$$a^{1/3} \times a^{1/3} \times a^{1/3} = a^{1/3 + 1/3 + 1/3} = a^1 = a$$
Therefore, by definition,
$$a^{1/3} = \sqrt[3]{a}$$

EXAMPLE 5

Evaluate: i) $(81)^{1/4}$
        ii) $4^{3/2}$

i)   Evaluate $81^{1/4}$

Using the rule for Fractional Powers we have
$$81^{1/4} = \sqrt[4]{81} = 3$$
(because $3 \times 3 \times 3 \times 3 = 81$)

31

ii)   Evaluate $4^{3/2}$

Again using the rule for Fractional Powers we have

$4^{3/2} = (\sqrt[2]{4})^3 = 2^3 = \mathbf{8}$

or, alternatively,

$4^{3/2} = \sqrt[2]{4^3} \;=\; \sqrt[2]{64} \;=\; \mathbf{8}$

EXERCISES   Questions similar to example 5.

Evaluate:

i) $9^{1/2}$
ii) $125^{1/3}$
iii) $256^{1/4}$
iv) $8^{2/3}$
v) $25^{3/2}$

EXAMPLE 6

Evaluate

$$64^{-2/3} \times 27^{4/3}$$

Using the rule for negative powers and the rule for fractional powers, we have:

$64^{-2/3} \times 27^{4/3}$

$$= \frac{1}{64^{2/3}} \times 27^{4/3} = \frac{1}{(\sqrt[3]{64})^2} \times (\sqrt[3]{27})^4$$

$$= \frac{1}{4^2} \times 3^4 = \frac{3^4}{4^2} = \frac{81}{16}$$

$$= 5\,\tfrac{1}{16}$$

EXAMPLE 7

Simplify

i) $4x^3y^5 \div x^2y^3$
ii) $a^{-3} \times a^5b^{-2}$
iii) $\left(\sqrt[4]{x^{-12}}\right)^5$

i) $4x^3y^5 \div x^2y^3 \;=\; \dfrac{4x^3y^5}{x^2y^3} = \mathbf{4xy^2}$

(we have divided both the numerator and the denominator by x^2y^3)

Alternatively, we could have used the division rule for powers as follows:

$4x^3y^5 \div x^2y^3 \;= 4x^{3-2}y^{5-3}$

$\qquad\qquad\qquad = \mathbf{4xy^2}$

ii) Using the multiplication rule for powers we have:
$$a^{-3} \times a^5 b^{-2} = a^{-3+5}b^{-2} = a^2 b^{-2}$$
$$= \frac{a^2}{b^2}$$

iii) $\left(\sqrt[4]{x^{-12}}\right)^5$

$= (x^{-12/4})^5$ *(using the rule for fractional powers)*
$= (x^{-3})^5$
$= x^{-15}$ *(using the rule for 'power of powers')*
$= \frac{1}{x^{15}}$

EXAMPLE 8

Simplify $\dfrac{(x^2)^3 \, (x^{-2})}{\sqrt[5]{x^3}}$

Let us first look at the numerator of this expression. We have:
$$(x^2)^3 \, (x^{-2}) = x^6 x^{-2} = x^4$$
Similarly, we now look at the denominator and we have:
$$\sqrt[5]{x^3} = x^{3/5}$$
Hence we now have
$$\frac{(x^2)^3 \, (x^{-2})}{\sqrt[5]{x^3}} = x^4 \div x^{3/5} = x^{4-\,3/5}$$
$$= x^{17/5}$$

$$= \sqrt[5]{x^{17}}$$

GENERAL EXERCISES

Evaluate the following:

i) $3^{12} \times 3^8$
ii) $(½)^4 \times (½)^3$
iii) $(-3)^2 \times (-3)^3$
iv) $2^5 \div 2^3$
v) $5^8 \div 5^7$
vi) $(¾)^{16} \div (¾)^{13}$
vii) 4^{-3}
viii) 2^{-5}
ix) $(-2)^3$
x) $6^5 \div 6^7$
xi) $(⅓)^2 \div (⅓)^3$

xii) $(-^2/5)^3 \div (-^2/5)^6$
xiii) $(-3^3)^2$
xiv) $64^{1/3}$
xv) $(-27)^{1/3}$
xvi) $16^{3/4}$
xvii) $27^{4/3}$
xviii) $(49^{1/2})^3$
xix) $4^{-3/2}$
xx) $27^{-2/3} + 9^{-1/2}$
xxi) $(^4/9)^{-1/2}$
xxii) $(^3/4)^{-2}$

Find k in each of the following:

xxiii) $3^4 \times 3^{1/2} = 3^k$
xxiv) $4^{1/2} \div 4^{-3/2} = 4^k$
xxv) $6^{-1/5} \div 6^{-1/10} = 6^k$
xxvi) $(5^2)^{1/4} \times (5^3)^{1/6} = 5^k$
xxvii) $9^3 \times 3^2 = 9^k$
xxviii) $(1000)^{2/3} = k$
xxix) $(4^3)^{-1/2} = k$
xxx) $\dfrac{16^{-1/2}}{25} = k$

Evaluate the following:

xxxi) $(^{16}/25)^{-1/2}$
xxxii) $4^{-1/2} \times 27^{-1/3}$
xxxiii) $(-4)^3 \times (-1)^5 \times (-½)^2$
xxxiv) $(-2)^2 \div (-4)^3$
xxxv) $(-4)^{-1/3} \div (-4)^{-2/3}$

Simplify the following:

xxxvi) $(\sqrt{x})^3$
xxxvii) $\left[\dfrac{1}{y^3}\right]^4$
xxxviii) $(x^2y)(3x^3y^4z)$
xxxix) $11a^2b^3 \times ab \times 3ab^2c^4$
xl) $4a^3yz^2 \div a^2y^2z$
xli) $m^2n \div mn^3$
xlii) $x^2y^{-3} \div \dfrac{x}{y}$
xliii) $(-18x^2y + 36x^3y - 9xy^2) \div 3x^2y^2$
xliv) $(4a^2b + 12ab^3 - 3a) \div 4b$
xlv) $(2pq - 4q^2 + 8p - 3p^3q^2) \div pq$

xlvi) $\dfrac{1}{[\sqrt[4]{x}]^2}$

xlvii) $\left[\sqrt{x^{-4}}\right]^9$

xlviii) $\dfrac{\left[x^4\right]^3 \left[\dfrac{1}{x^7}\right]^5}{(\sqrt[3]{x})^6}$

UNIT 5 – POWERS
SOLUTIONS TO EXERCISES

1. Questions similar to example 1.
    i) 2^8
    ii) 4^9
    iii) $(3\,\tfrac{1}{2})^7$
    iv) x^{11}
    v) q^{a+b}

2. Questions similar to example 2.
    i) 3^3
    ii) 5^6
    iii) 12.75
    vi) x^{11}
    v) y^4

3. Questions similar to example 3.
    i) $1/25$
    ii) $1/81$
    iii) $2^{-2} = 1/4$
    iv) $4^{-3} = 1/64$
    v) $x^{-1} = \dfrac{1}{x}$
    vi) $p^{-4} = \dfrac{1}{p^4}$

4. Questions similar to example 4.
    i) $3^4 = 81$
    ii) 4^9
    iii) 10^8
    iv) x^{20}
    v) z^{14}

5. Questions similar to example 5.
   - i)   3
   - ii)   5
   - iii)   4
   - iv)   4
   - v)   125

6. General Exercises
   - i) 3^{20}
   - ii) $(\frac{1}{2})^7$
   - iii) $(-3)^5$
   - iv)   4
   - v)   5
   - vi) $(\frac{3}{4})^3$
   - vii) $1/64$
   - viii) $1/32$
   - ix) -8
   - x) $1/36$
   - xi)   3
   - xii) $(-2/5)^{-3} = -125/8$
   - xiii)   729
   - xiv)   4
   - xv) -3
   - xvi)   8
   - xvii)   81
   - xviii)   343
   - xix) $\frac{1}{8}$
   - xx) $4/9$
   - xxi) $3/2$
   - xxii) $1\,7/9$
   - xxiii) $4\frac{1}{2}$
   - xxiv)   2
   - xxv) $-1/10$
   - xxvi)   1
   - xxvii)   4
   - xxviii)   100
   - xxix) $\frac{1}{8}$
   - xxx) $1/100$
   - xxxi) $5/4$
   - xxxii) $1/6$
   - xxxiii)   16
   - xxxiv) $-1/16$
   - xxxv) $(-4)^{1/3}$
   - xxxvi) $x^{3/2}$
   - xxxvii) $y^{-12} = \dfrac{1}{y^{12}}$

xxxviii) $3x^5y^5z$

xxxix) $33a^4b^6c^4$

xl) $\dfrac{4az}{y}$

xli) $\dfrac{m}{n^2}$

xlii) $\dfrac{x}{y^2}$

xliii) $-\dfrac{6}{y} + \dfrac{12x}{y} - \dfrac{3}{x}$

xliv) $a^2 + 3ab^2 - \dfrac{3a}{4b}$

xlv) $2 - \dfrac{4q}{p} + \dfrac{8}{q} - 3p^2q$

xlvi) $x^{-1/2} = \dfrac{1}{\sqrt{x}}$

xlvii) $x^{-18} = \dfrac{1}{x^{18}}$

xlviii) $x^{-25} = \dfrac{1}{x^{25}}$

6. COORDINATES AND GRAPHS

COORDINATES

An equation involving two variables can be represented by a graph drawn on 'Coordinates Axes'. Coordinate axes (illustrated below) consist of a horizontal line (usually referred to as the x axis) and a vertical line (usually referred to as the y axis). The point of intersection of these two lines is called the origin (usually denoted by the letter 'O').

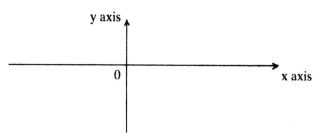

Along the x and y axes we can mark off units of measurement (not necessarily the same on both axes). The origin takes the value zero on both axes. The x axis takes positive values to the right of the origin and negative values to the left of the origin. The y axis takes positive values above the origin and negative values below the origin.

Any point on this diagram can be defined by its coordinates (consisting of two numbers). The first, the x coordinate, is defined as the horizontal distance of the point from the y axis; the second, the y coordinate, is defined as the vertical distance of the point from the x axis.

In general, a point is defined by its coordinates which are written in the form (a, b).

EXAMPLE 1

The point (3, 2) may be plotted on the coordinate axes as follows:-

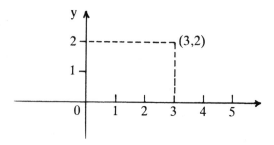

EXAMPLE 2

Consider the following diagram

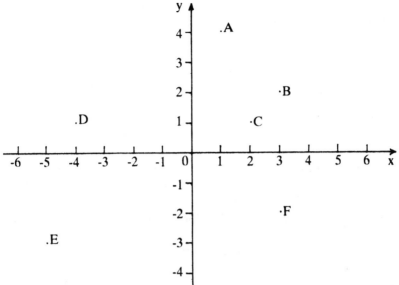

The points A, B, C, D, E and F above are defined by their coordinates as follows:

A	(1, 4)	D	(–4, 1)
B	(3, 2)	E	(–5, –3)
C	(2, 1)	F	(3, –2)

EXERCISES   Questions similar to examples 1 and 2.

Plot the following points on coordinate axes.

i)	(2, 3)	ii)	(1, 4)	iii)	(5, 0)
iv)	(0, 2)	v)	(3, –1)	vi)	(–2, 4)
vii)	(–1, –3)	viii)	(0, –4)	ix)	(–5, 0)
x)	(–4, 1)	xi)	(–3, –1)	xii)	(3, –3)

GRAPHS

An equation involving two variables can be represented, on co-ordinate axes, by means of a graph.

For a given range of values of x, the corresponding y values can be calculated from the equation being considered. The points obtained can then be plotted and joined together to form the graph.

Before plotting the points on a graph, the axes must be drawn in a way that takes into account the range of the x-values and the range of the y-values. If graph paper is used (which is desirable) you should use a scale that involves a sensible number of units per square i.e. you should use steps of, for example, 1, 2, 5 or 10 etc. units per square depending on the question. You should avoid using steps along the axes of, for example, 7 or 9 units per square as this can complicate the graph unnecessarily.

39

EXAMPLE 3

Draw the graph of $y = 2x + 1$ for $0 \leqslant x \leqslant 5$.

By taking x values of 0, 1, 2, ... 5, we can calculate the corresponding y values, as shown below, by first evaluating the component parts of the equation.

x:	0	1	2	3	4	5
2x	0	2	4	6	8	10
+1	1	1	1	1	1	1
y:	1	3	5	7	9	11

We then plot the points obtained, each point being defined by its x coordinate and its correspoinding y coordinate. The points are then joined together to form the graph.

In this example the points to be plotted are (0, 1), (1, 3), (2, 5), (3, 7), (4, 9), (5, 11).

Graph of $y = 2x + 1$

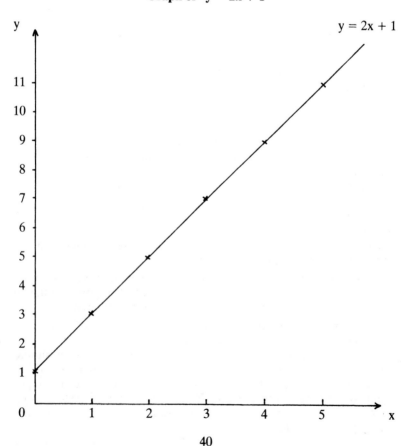

EXAMPLE 4

Draw a graph of $y = x^2 - 8x + 12$ for $0 \leqslant x \leqslant 6$

We again take x values covering the given range, and calculate the corresponding y values from the given equation.

x:	0	1	2	3	4	5	6
x^2	0	1	4	9	16	25	36
$-8x$	0	-8	-16	-24	-32	-40	-48
$+12$	+12	+12	+12	+12	+12	+12	+12
y:	12	5	0	-3	-4	-3	0

We now plot the points obtained and join them together to form the graph. In this example the points to be plotted are $(0, 12)$, $(1, 5)$, $(2, 0)$, $(3, -3)$, $(4, -4)$, $(5, -3)$, $(6, 0)$.

Graph of $y = x^2 - 8x + 12$

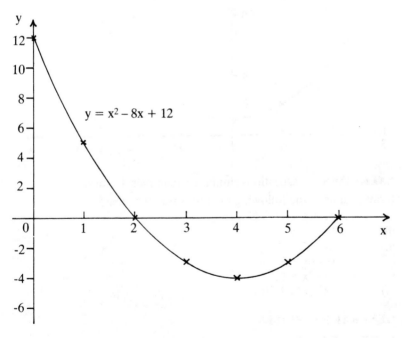

N.B. For a more detailed graph we could, of course, include more points. e.g. by taking x values of

$$0, \; \tfrac{1}{2}, \; 1, \; 1\tfrac{1}{2}, \; 2, \; 2\tfrac{1}{2}, \; \ldots\ldots\ldots\; 5\tfrac{1}{2}, \; 6$$

and calculating the corresponding y values, we could plot nearly twice as many points as we did in the above example

EXAMPLE 5

Draw a graph of $y = x^2 + 1$ for $-3 \leqslant x \leqslant +3$

Again, taking x values covering the given range, we first calculate the corresponding y values from the given equation.

x:	-3	-2	-1	0	1	2	3
x^2	9	4	1	0	1	4	9
$+1$	$+1$	$+1$	$+1$	$+1$	$+1$	$+1$	$+1$
y:	10	5	2	1	2	5	10

We now plot the points obtained and join them together to form the graph.

Graph of $y = x^2 + 1$

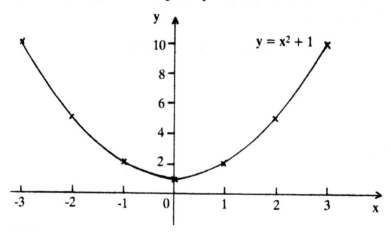

EXERCISES   Questions similar to examples 3, 4 and 5.

Draw graphs of the following functions for $0 \leqslant x \leqslant 5$

i) $y = 2x + 5$
ii) $y = 5x + 1$
iii) $y = 3x - 5$
iv) $y = x^2 - 6x + 5$
v) $y = x^2 - 7x + 12$
vi) $y = 3x^2 - 21x + 30$

GENERAL EXERCISES

EXERCISE 1

Plot the following points on coordinate axes:

i) $(1, \ 3)$ ii) $(4, \ 1)$
iii) $(-1, \ 4)$ iv) $(-3, \ 4)$

v)	(5, −3)	vi)	(5, −1)
vii)	(−1, −1)	viii)	(−4, 0)
ix)	(0, 4)	x)	(−3, −5)

EXERCISE 2

Draw graphs of the following functions for $-3 \leqslant x \leqslant 3$

i) $y = 2x^2 + 7$
ii) $y = 3x^2 - 12$
iii) $y = x^3 - 7$
iv) $y = 4x^3 - 16x^2 - 16x + 64$
v) $y = \dfrac{1}{x + 5}$

UNIT 6 – COORDINATES & GRAPHS
SOLUTIONS TO EXERCISES

1.   Questions similar to examples 1 and 2.

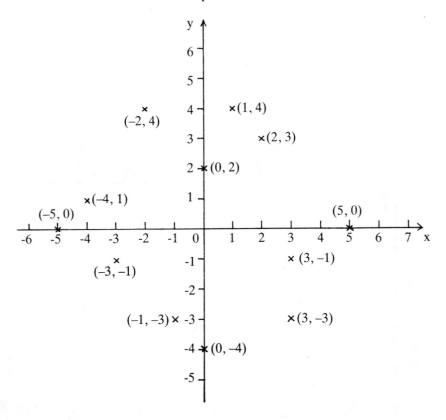

2.   Questions similar to examples 3, 4 and 5.

i)   y = 2x + 5

x:	0	1	2	3	4	5
y:	5	7	9	11	13	15

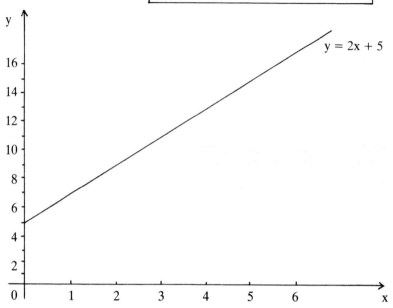

ii)   y = 5x + 1

x:	0	1	2	3	4	5
y:	1	6	11	16	21	26

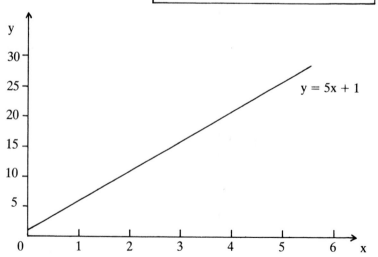

iii) $y = 3x - 5$

x:	0	1	2	3	4	5
y:	−5	−2	1	4	7	10

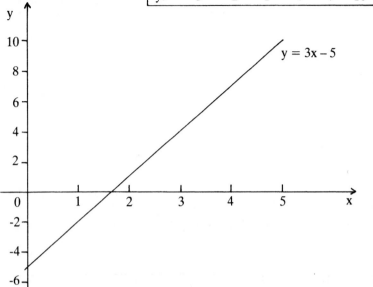

iv) $y = x^2 - 6x + 5$

x:	0	1	2	3	4	5
y:	5	0	−3	−4	−3	0

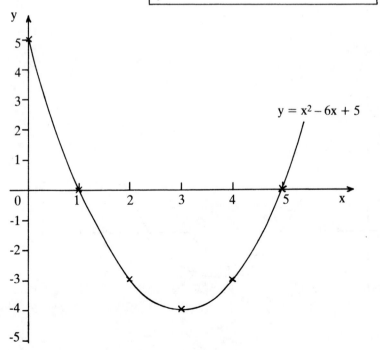

45

v) $y = x^2 - 7x + 12$

x:	0	1	2	3	4	5
y:	12	6	2	0	0	2

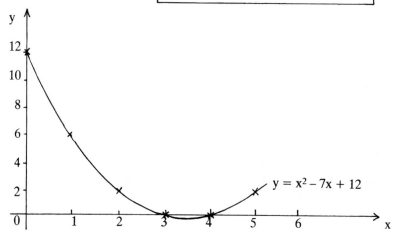

vi) $y = 3x^2 - 21x + 30$

x:	0	1	2	3	4	5
y:	30	12	0	-6	-6	0

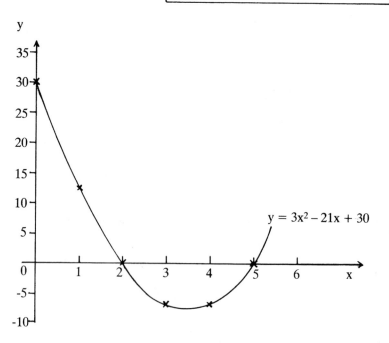

46

3. General Exercises

EXERCISE 1

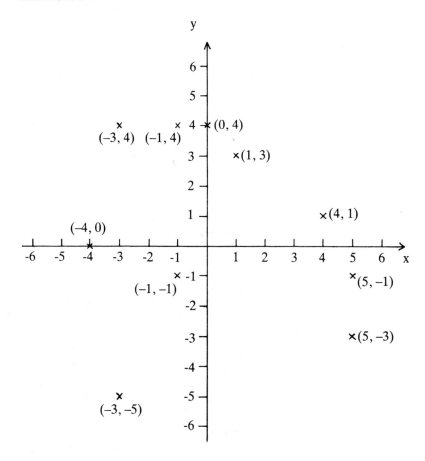

EXERCISE 2

i) $y = 2x^2 + 7$

x:	−3	−2	−1	0	1	2	3
y:	25	15	9	7	9	15	25

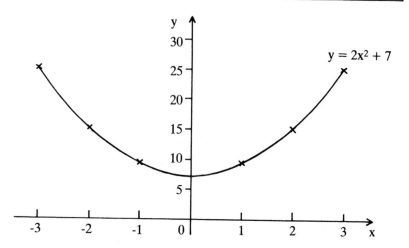

ii) $y = 3x^2 - 12$

x:	−3	−2	−1	0	1	2	3
y:	15	0	−9	−12	−9	0	15

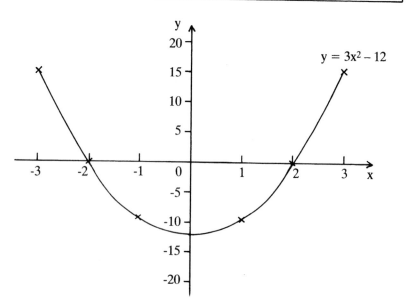

iii) $y = x^3 - 7$

x:	−3	−2	−1	0	1	2	3
y:	−34	−15	−8	−7	−6	1	20

$y = x^3 - 7$

iv) $y = 4x^3 - 16x^2 - 16x + 64$

x:	−3	−2	−1	0	1	2	3
y:	−140	0	60	64	36	0	−20

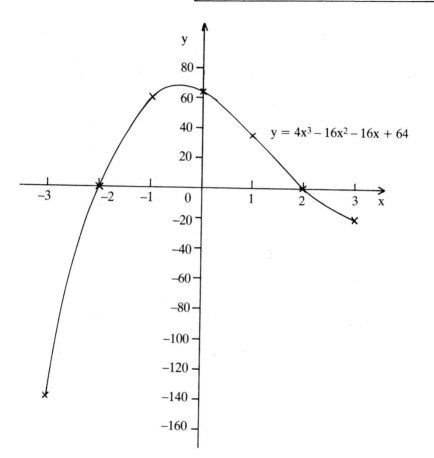

$y = 4x^3 - 16x^2 - 16x + 64$

v) $y = \dfrac{1}{x + 5}$

x:	−3	−2	−1	0	1	2	3
y:	½	⅓	¼	⅕	⅙	⅐	⅛

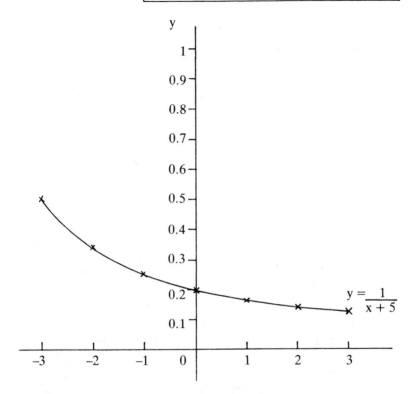

$y = \dfrac{1}{x + 5}$

7. THE STRAIGHT LINE

INTRODUCTION

A straight line is defined as the shortest distance between two points.
The equation of a straight line is given by

$$y = mx + c$$

where m represents the slope of the line and c is the point where
the line crosses the y axis (i.e. the y intercept). The point where the line
crosses the x axis is called the x intercept.

EXAMPLE 1

Graph of y = 2x

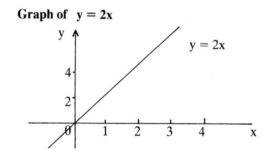

In this example, m = 2 and c = 0
Note that whenever c = 0, the line will pass through the origin.

EXAMPLE 2

Graph of y = 6 – 3x

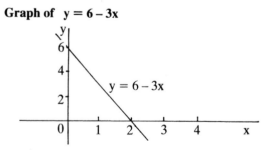

In this example, m = – 3 and c = 6

As c = 6, we know that this line cuts the y axis at y = 6 (this can be
verified by substituting x = 0 into the equation of the line, as x = 0
along the y axis).

Similarly, as y = 0 along the x axis, we can substitute y = 0 into the
equation of the line to find where the line intersects with the x axis (i.e.
the x intercept).

We have, when y = 0

$$6 - 3x = 0$$
$$3x = 6$$
$$x = 2$$

Hence the line cuts the x axis at x = 2

We can now say that

the y intercept = 6
and the x intercept = 2

EXAMPLE 3

Graph of y = – 2 + 4x

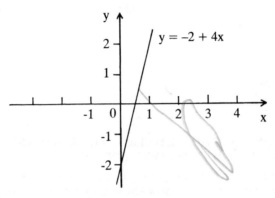

In this example, m = 4 and c = – 2

We know, immediately, that the y intercept is – 2 (i.e. the value of c)

To find the x intercept, we substitute y = 0 into the equation of the line.

i.e.

$$0 = -2 + 4x$$
$$4x = +2$$
$$x = +\tfrac{1}{2}$$

Hence the x intercept is x = ½

EXAMPLE 4 – SPECIAL CASES

A straight line parallel to the x axis takes the form y = constant.

Similarily, a straight line parallel to the y axis takes the form x = constant.

These cases are illustrated below:

Straight line parallel to the x axis   **Straight line parallel to the y axis**

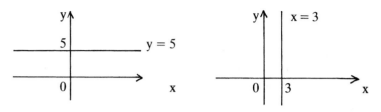

EXERCISES   Questions similar to examples 1, 2, 3 and 4.

For each of the following equations identify the values of m and c and then draw the graph.

i) $y = 4x + 5$
ii) $y = 9x$
iii) $y = 8$
iv) $y = 4/5 - 3x/7$
v) $y = \dfrac{6 - 5x}{13}$

DERIVATION OF THE EQUATION OF A STRAIGHT LINE PASSING THROUGH TWO GIVEN POINTS.

Given the coordinates of two points, (x_1, y_1) and (x_2, y_2) say, we can calculate the equation of the straight line that passes through these points.

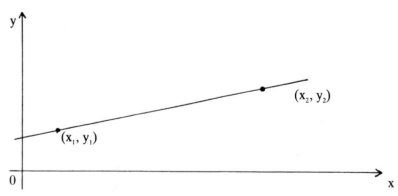

Two methods of calculating this equation are illustrated below:

EXAMPLE 5

The question is: Find the equation of the straight line that passes through the points (1, 4) and (3, 10).

54

Method 1

The general equation of a straight line is given by

$$y = mx + c$$

and it is necessary to find numerical values for m and c.

If the straight line in question passes through the two given points, then each of these points must satisfy the equation of this straight line. That is, we can substitute the coordinates of each point as follows:

$$y = mx + c$$

substituting $(1, 4)$ we have

$$4 = m + c \dots\dots\dots\dots (1)$$

likewise, substituting $(3, 10)$ we have

$$10 = 3m + c \dots\dots\dots\dots (2)$$

Now (1) and (2) give us two equations in two unknowns, m and c, (i.e. simultaneous equations) which we can solve.

We have

$$4 = m + c \dots\dots\dots\dots (1)$$
$$10 = 3m + c \dots\dots\dots\dots (2)$$

subtracting (1) from (2) to eliminate c we obtain

$$6 = 2m$$
$$\mathbf{m = 3}$$

substituting this value of m back into (1) we obtain

$$4 = m + c$$
$$4 = 3 + c$$
$$c = 4 - 3$$
$$\mathbf{c = 1}$$

If we now substitute these numerical values of m and c into the equation $y = mx + c$, we obtain the equation of the straight line passing throught the points $(1, 4)$ and $(3, 10)$.

That is

$$\mathbf{y = 3x + 1}$$

Method 2

In general, we can consider any two points (x_1, y_1) and (x_2, y_2). The straight line passing through these points can be written as

$$y - y_1 = m(x - x_1)$$

where $m = \dfrac{y_2 - y_1}{x_2 - x_1}$ (m is the gradient of the line)

Applying this to the points $(1, 4)$ and $(3, 10)$ we have

$$x_1 = 1; \, y_1 = 4; \, x_2 = 3; \, y_2 = 10;$$

and we hence obtain:

$$m = \frac{10-4}{3-1} = \frac{6}{2} = 3$$

and our line becomes

$$y - 4 = 3(x - 1)$$
$$y - 4 = 3x - 3$$
$$y = 3x + 1$$

N.B. In this example, the point (1, 4) corresponded to (x_1, y_1) and the point (3, 10) corresponded to (x_2, y_2).

If we had worked through this example with the point (3, 10) corresponding to (x_1, y_1), and the point (1, 4) corresponding to (x_2, y_2), the answer would have been exactly the same.

EXERCISES   Questions similar to example 5.

Calculate the equation of the straight line that passes through the following points.

i)   (1, 3) and (3, 7)
ii)   (0, 2) and (5, 22)
iii)   (1, −5) and (−1, −9)

GENERAL EXERCISES

Draw a graph of the following straight lines indicating where they cross the axes:

i) $y = 7x$
ii) $y = 4x + 3$
iii) $y = 2x - 1$
iv) $y = 2 - 3x$
v) $y = -3x - 7$

Calculate the equation of the straight line that passes through the following points:

vi)   (1, 7) and (3, 11)
vii)   (0, 0) and (1, 6)
viii)   (3, −2) and (2, 1)
ix)   (0, 0) and (−2, 8)
x)   (6, 1) and (4, −1)
xi)   (0, −3) and (−2, 1)
xii)   (2, 6) and (7, 6)
xiii)   (−5, −47) and (−2, −26)
xiv)   (3, 1) and (3, −2)
xv)   (1, 1¼) and (2, 2¾)

UNIT 7 - THE STRAIGHT LINE
SOLUTIONS TO EXERCISES

1. Questions similar to examples 1, 2, 3 and 4.

   i)   m = 4, c = 5

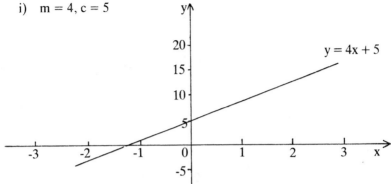

   ii)   m = 9, c = 0

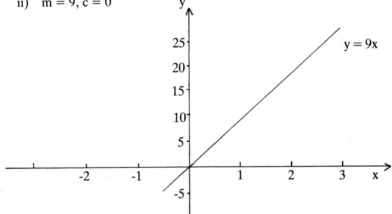

   iii)   m = 0, c = 8

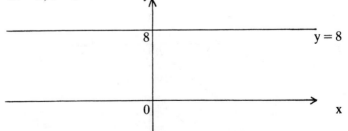

iv) $m = -3/7, c = 4/5$

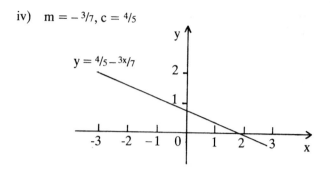

$$y = 4/5 - 3x/7$$

v) $m = -5/13, c = 6/13$

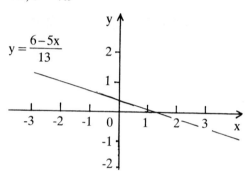

$$y = \frac{6-5x}{13}$$

2. Questions similar to example 5.
   i) $y = 2x + 1$
   ii) $y = 4x + 2$
   iii) $y = 2x - 7$

3. General Exercises
   i)

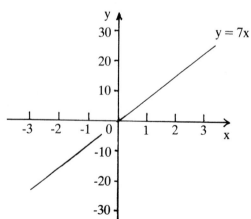

$$y = 7x$$

This line crosses the axes at the origin.

ii)

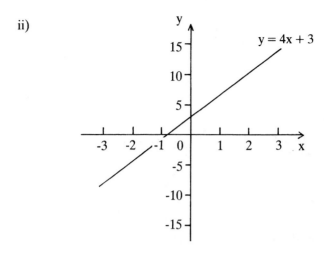

This line crosses the axes at x = $-\frac{3}{4}$ and y = 3.

iii)

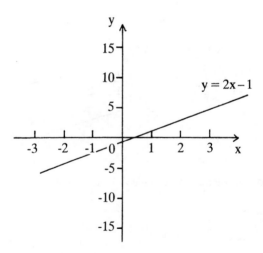

This line crosses the axes at x = $\frac{1}{2}$ and y = -1.

iv)

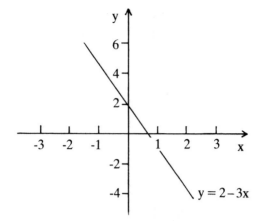

This line crosses the axes at x = ⅔ and y = 2.

v)

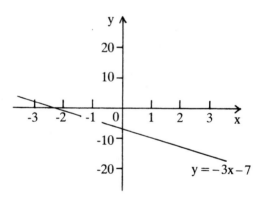

This line crosses the axes at x = –2 ⅓ and y = – 7.

vi)   y = 2x + 5
vii)   y = 6x
viii)   y = 7 – 3x
ix)   y = – 4x
x)   y = x – 5
xi)   y = – 2x – 3
xii)   y = 6
xiii)   y = 7x – 12
xiv)   x = 3
xv)   y = ³ˣ/₂ – ¼

8. SIMPLE LINEAR EQUATIONS

INTRODUCTION

Any statement of equality between two quantities is an equation. This unit is concerned with the solution of equations that can be rearranged into the form

$$ax + b = 0$$

where x is the unknown (variable), and a and b are constants.

To solve equations of this form [i.e. to find the value of the unknown (variable) in the equation], we may first need to manipulate the equation so that all the terms involving the unknown (variable) appear on one side of the equation, and only constants appear on the other side.

N.B. When manipulating the terms of an equation it must remembered that whatever arithmetic operation is performed to one side of the equation must also be performed to the other side.

Examples of the solution of such equations are given below.

EXAMPLE 1

Solve $2x - 4 = 10$

We want to find the numerical value of x that satisfies this equation.

By moving $- 4$ to the R.H.S. of the equation, remembering that we must change the sign (i.e. by adding $+ 4$ to both sides of the equation) we obtain

$$2x = 10 + 4$$
$$2x = 14$$

now, by dividing both sides of the equation by 2, we obtain

$$\frac{2x}{2} = \frac{14}{2}$$

$$x = 7$$

Hence $x = 7$ is the solution to the equation $2x - 4 = 10$.

We can check our answer by substituting it back into the original equation

i.e. $2x - 4 = 10$
$2(7) - 4 = 10$
$14 - 4 = 10$

Since this is true, our solution is correct.

EXERCISES   Questions similar to example 1.

Solve the following:

i) $x - 3 = 4$
ii) $3x - 5 = 7$
iii) $2 - x = 1$
iv) $14 - 5x = -6$
v) $-3 + 4x = 5$

EXAMPLE 2

Solve $3x - 2 = 2x + 4$

We aim to get the terms in x on one side of the equation and the constants on the other.

Now, by moving -2 to the R.H.S. of the equation (i.e. by adding $+2$ to both sides of the equation), we obtain

$$3x = 2x + 4 + 2$$
$$3x = 2x + 6$$

Now by moving 2x to the L.H.S. of the equation (i.e. by subtracting 2x from both sides of the equation), we obtain

$$3x - 2x = 6$$
$$\mathbf{x = 6}$$

This is the solution and we can check it by substituting back into the original equation.

i.e. $3x - 2 = 2x + 4$
       $3(6) - 2 = 2(6) + 4$
       $18 - 2 = 12 + 4$
       $16 = 16$

Since this is true, our solution is correct.

EXERCISES   Questions similar to example 2.

Solve the following

i) $4x + 1 = 3x + 2$
ii) $2 - x = 7x - 6$
iii) $4 + 2x = 5x - 8$
iv) $-4 - 3x = -7 - 2x$
v) $5x - 2 = -12x - 36$

EXAMPLE 3

Solve $\dfrac{4x}{5} = 1$

By multiplying both sides of the equation by 5, we obtain

$$5\left[\frac{4x}{5}\right] = 5(1)$$
$$4x = 5$$

by dividing both sides of the equation by 4, we obtain

$$\frac{4x}{4} = \frac{5}{4}$$

$$x = {}^5/_4$$

$$x = 1\,\tfrac{1}{4}$$

We can check this answer by substituting it back into the original equation

i.e.
$$\frac{4x}{5} = 1$$

$${}^4/_5(1\,\tfrac{1}{4}) = 1$$

$${}^4/_5({}^5/_4) = 1$$

Since this is true our solution is correct.

EXERCISES   Questions similar to example 3.

Solve the following:

i) ${}^{8x}/_3 = 16$

ii) $1\,\tfrac{3}{4}\,x = -7$

iii) $-\,{}^{2x}/_3 = -6$

iv) $-3\,\tfrac{2}{3}\,x = 4$

v) ${}^{7x}/_5 = -1$

EXAMPLE 4

Solve $\tfrac{1}{2}\,(3x - 1) = 7$

This equation can be written as

$$\frac{3x - 1}{2} = 7$$

multiplying both sides of the equation by 2, we obtain

$$2\left[\frac{3x - 1}{2}\right] = 2(7)$$

$$3x - 1 = 14$$

by moving -1 to the R.H.S. of the equation (i.e. by adding $+1$ to both sides of the equation), we obtain

$$3x = 14 + 1$$

$$3x = 15$$

by dividing both sides of the equation by 3, we obtain

$$\frac{3x}{3} = \frac{15}{3}$$

$$x = 5$$

This is the solution.

EXERCISES   Questions similar to example 4.

Solve the following:

i) $2(3x - 1) = 28$
ii) $5(3 - 2x) = 35$
iii) $3(2x + 1) = -15$
iv) $-4(1 - x) = 24$
v) $\frac{3}{4}(5 - 3x) = 15$

EXAMPLE 5

Solve $\frac{2}{3}(x - 1) = \frac{4}{5}(2x - 3)$

This equation can be written as

$$\frac{2(x - 1)}{3} = \frac{4(2x - 3)}{5}$$

Using the process of cross-multiplication, we obtain

$$5[2(x - 1)] = 3[4(2x - 3)]$$
$$10(x - 1) = 12(2x - 3)$$

eliminating the brackets, we obtain

$$10x - 10 = 24x - 36$$

rearranging the equation so that the terms in x are on the R.H.S. of the equation, and the constants are on the L.H.S., we obtain

$$-10 + 36 = 24x - 10x$$
$$26 = 14x$$

dividing both sides of the equation by 14, we obtain

$$\frac{26}{14} = \frac{14x}{14}$$

$$\frac{26}{14} = x$$

$$x = 1\,\frac{6}{7}$$

This is the solution.

EXERCISES   Questions similar to example 5.

Solve the following

i) $\frac{2}{3}(x - 3) = \frac{1}{2}(x - 1)$
ii) $1\frac{1}{4}(4 - 2x) = \frac{5}{14}(6x + 1)$
iii) $\frac{3}{2}(x - 2) = \frac{4}{3}(3 - 2x)$
vi) $-\frac{2}{3}(x - 3) = 4x$
v) $2\frac{2}{5}(x - 3) = -\frac{3x}{4}$

EXAMPLE 6

Solve

$$9\left(\frac{x+3}{10}\right) + \frac{7}{2} = \frac{5x}{2} + 3(x-1)$$

In order to first simplify this equation we can multiply both sides of the equation by 10, thus eliminating the denominators.
We then have:

$$10\left[9\left(\frac{x+3}{10}\right) + \frac{7}{2}\right] = 10\left[\frac{5x}{2} + 3(x-1)\right]$$

Expanding the brackets we have:

$$9(x+3) + 35 = 25x + 30(x-1)$$
$$9x + 27 + 35 = 25x + 30x - 30$$
$$9x + 62 = 55x - 30$$

Rearranging the equation so that the terms in x are on the R.H.S. of the equation, we have:

$$30 + 62 = 55x - 9x$$
$$92 = 46x$$
$$\mathbf{x = 2}$$

GENERAL EXERCISES

Solve the following:

i) $3x = x - 7$
ii) $2(3-2x) = -2$
iii) $x - 2 = 7 - 2x$
iv) $x/5 = -2$
v) $x/4 + 3 = 2\frac{1}{2}$
vi) $x/2 - \frac{1}{4} = 3x/4 + 1$
vii) $\frac{2}{3}(2-3x) = x/6 - \frac{5}{6}$
viii) $2(3a-1) = 5(a+7)$
ix) $1/y = 5$
x) $\dfrac{2}{3x} = \dfrac{1}{6}$

xi) $\dfrac{1}{k-3} = \dfrac{2}{k+5}$

xii) $\dfrac{2}{3-x} = 3$

xiii) $\dfrac{1}{2x-4} = \dfrac{3}{2(1-4x)}$

xiv) $\dfrac{3}{4x} = \dfrac{2}{3x+1}$

xv) $3(67/6 - 5x) = \dfrac{x}{4} + 3$

65

xvi) $2(3t + 7) + 4(8 - t) = 8(t + 2)$

xvii) $\frac{3}{4} + 2(3 - z) = \frac{1}{2}(2 - 6z)$

xviii) $\frac{1}{2}\left[2x + \frac{1}{3}(x - 3)\right] = \frac{4x}{3} + 7$

xix) $\dfrac{3x^2 - 7x}{x} = 2$

xx) $3\left[\dfrac{4x - 7}{2}\right] = 5(x - 2) + \dfrac{x}{4} + 3$

UNIT 8 – SIMPLE LINEAR EQUATIONS
SOLUTIONS TO EXERCISES

1. Questions similar to example 1.

   i) $x = 7$
   ii) $x = 4$
   iii) $x = 1$
   iv) $x = 4$
   v) $x = 2$

2. Questions similar to example 2.

   i) $x = 1$
   ii) $x = 1$
   iii) $x = 4$
   vi) $x = 3$
   v) $x = -2$

3. Questions similar to example 3.

   i) $x = 6$
   ii) $x = -4$
   iii) $x = 9$
   iv) $x = -\,^{12}/_{11}$
   v) $x = -\,^{5}/_{7}$

4. Questions similar to example 4.

   i) $x = 5$
   ii) $x = -2$
   iii) $x = -3$
   iv) $x = 7$
   v) $x = -5$

5. Questions similar to example 5.

   i) $x = 9$
   ii) $x = 1$
   iii) $x = 1\,^{17}/_{25}$
   iv) $x = \,^{3}/_{7}$
   v) $x = 2\,^{6}/_{21}$

6. General Exercises

i)	$x = -3\frac{1}{2}$
ii)	$x = 2$
iii)	$x = 3$
iv)	$x = -10$
v)	$x = -2$
vi)	$x = -5$
vii)	$x = 1$
viii)	$a = 37$
ix)	$y = \frac{1}{5}$
x)	$x = 4$
xi)	$k = 11$
xii)	$x = 2\frac{1}{3}$
xiii)	$x = 1$
xiv)	$x = -3$
xv)	$x = 2$
xvi)	$t = 5$
xvii)	$z = -5\frac{3}{4}$
xviii)	$x = -45$
xix)	$x = 3$
xx)	$x = 4\frac{2}{3}$

9. SIMULTANEOUS EQUATIONS

INTRODUCTION

This unit is concerned with the solution of two linear equations in two unknowns (variables) i.e. finding the values of the two unknowns (variables) which simultaneously satisfy the two equations in question. Generally, if a problem involves more than one unknown, a unique solution is obtainable only if

a)   There are as many equations as there are unknowns
b)   The equations are consistent
c)   The equations are independent

The following equations are *inconsistent* because x and y cannot satisfy both equations.

i) $x + y = 1$
ii) $x + y = 2$

The following equations are *dependent* because the second equation is simply a multiple of the first equation.

i) $x + y = 1$
ii) $2x + 2y = 2$

The solution of a pair of simultaneous equations occurs at the intersection of the graph of the two equations.

The examples below illustrate methods of solution of simultaneous linear equations.

EXAMPLE 1

Solve $x + y = 2$
               $2x + y = 3$

a)   by elimination
b)   by substitution
c)   graphically

a) $x + y = 2$ .... (i)
               $2x + y = 3$ .... (ii)

subtracting equation (i) from equation (ii), term by term, we obtain

$$(2x - x) + (y - y) = 3 - 2$$

Hence $x = 1$

We can now substitute this value of x into either of the original equations i.e. (i) or (ii).

68

If we substitute into equation (i) we obtain

$$x + y = 2$$
$$1 + y = 2$$
$$y = 2 - 1$$
$$\mathbf{y = 1}$$

Hence the solution is $\mathbf{x = 1 \quad y = 1}$

b)
$$x + y = 2 \ldots\ldots\ldots\ldots \text{(i)}$$
$$2x + y = 3 \ldots\ldots\ldots\ldots \text{(ii)}$$

We can rewrite equation (i) as follows:

$$x + y = 2$$
$$y = 2 - x$$

If we now substitute this into (ii) we obtain

$$2x + y = 3 \ldots\ldots\ldots\ldots \text{(ii)}$$
$$2x + (2 - x) = 3$$
$$2x + 2 - x = 3$$
$$x + 2 = 3$$
$$x = 3 - 2$$
$$\mathbf{x = 1}$$

Now substituting this value of x into (i) we obtain

$$x + y = 2$$
$$1 + y = 2$$
$$y = 2 - 1$$
$$\mathbf{y = 1}$$

Hence we obtain the solution $\mathbf{x = 1 \quad y = 1}$

c)
$$x + y = 2 \ldots\ldots\ldots\ldots \text{(i)}$$
$$2x + y = 3 \ldots\ldots\ldots\ldots \text{(ii)}$$

We want to graph the two equations on the same axis.

First we can rewrite the equations in a more suitable form as follows:

$$\text{equation (i) becomes} \quad y = 2 - x$$
$$\text{and equation (ii) becomes} \quad y = 3 - 2x$$

The equations, written in this form, are easier to graph.

The graphs are given below:

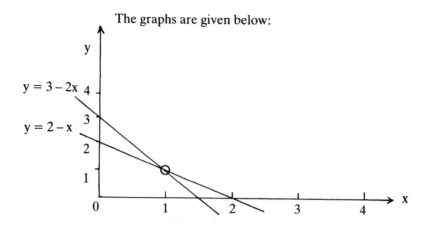

The two graphs intersect at the point **x = 1, y = 1**. This, therefore, is the solution.

We can always check our solution by substituting it back into the original equations.

That is, we have calculated the solution of

$$x + y = 2 \ \text{.................} \ (i)$$
$$2x + y = 3 \ \text{.................} \ (ii)$$

to be

$$x = 1, y = 1$$

then by substituting these values of x and y into (i) and (ii).

we have

$$1 + 1 = 2 \ \text{............} \ (i)$$
$$2(1) + 1 = 3 \ \text{............} \ (ii)$$

both of which are correct. Therefore our solution is correct.

EXAMPLE 2

Solve $3x + 2y = 4 \text{..........} (i)$
$4x + \ y = 7 \text{..........} (ii)$

The solution of these equations will again be illustrated by elimination, by substitution and graphically.

a)   solution by elimination

The first step is to ensure that either the coefficients of the x's are the same OR the coefficients of the y's are the same in both equations (regardless of sign).

If we multiply equation (ii) by 2, then the coefficients of the y's will be the same in both equations and we obtain

$$3x + 2y = 4 \ldots\ldots\ldots (i)$$
$$8x + 2y = 14 \ldots\ldots\ldots (ii) \text{ multiplied by } 2$$

subtracting these two equations, term by term, we eliminate the terms in y and hence obtain

$$(8x - 3x) + (2y - 2y) = 14 - 4$$
$$5x = 10$$
$$\mathbf{x = 2}$$

Substituting this value of x into either of our original equations, say equation (i), we obtain

$$3x + 2y = 4$$
$$3(2) + 2y = 4$$
$$6 + 2y = 4$$
$$2y = 4 - 6 = -2$$
$$\mathbf{y = -1}$$

Hence the solution is

$$\mathbf{x = 2, \quad y = -1}$$

b) solution by substitution

$$3x + 2y = 4 \ldots\ldots (i)$$
$$4x + y = 7 \ldots\ldots (ii)$$

We can rewrite equation (ii) as follows:

$$4x + y = 7$$
$$y = 7 - 4x$$

If we now substitute this into (i) we obtain

$$3x + 2y = 4$$
$$3x + 2(7 - 4x) = 4$$
$$3x + 14 - 8x = 4$$
$$14 - 5x = 4$$
$$14 - 4 = 5x$$
$$10 = 5x$$
$$\mathbf{x = 2}$$

Substituting this value of x into either of our original equations, say equation (i), we obtain

$$3x + 2y = 4$$
$$3(2) + 2y = 4$$
$$6 + 2y = 4$$
$$2y = 4 - 6 = -2$$
$$\mathbf{y = -1}$$

c) Graphical Solution

$$3x + 2y = 4 \ldots\ldots \text{(i)}$$
$$4x + y = 7 \ldots\ldots \text{(ii)}$$

We want to graph the two equations on the same axis.

First we can rewrite the equations in a more suitable form as follows:

equation (i) becomes $y = 2 - \frac{3x}{2}$
and equation (ii) becomes $y = 7 - 4x$

The graphs of the two equations are given below.

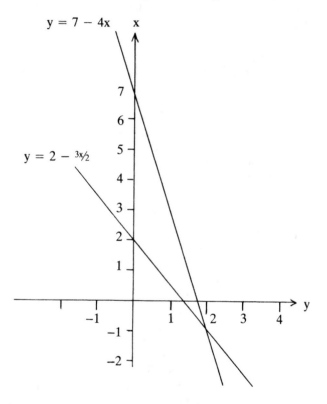

The two graphs intersect at the point

$$x = 2, \quad y = -1$$

This, therefore, is the solution.

Again, we can check this solution by substituting it back into the original equations (i) and (ii).

We thus obtain

$$3(2) + 2(-1) = 4 .... (i)$$
$$4(2) + (-1) = 7 .... (ii)$$

i.e.

$$6 - 2 = 4$$
$$\text{and} \quad 8 - 1 = 7$$

which are both correct. Therefore our solution is correct.

EXAMPLE 3

$$\text{Solve} \quad -3x + 2y = 1 \quad .... \text{(i)}$$
$$x + 3y = 18 .... \text{(ii)}$$

Using the elimination method, which is perhaps the most commonly used method, we can multiply (ii) by 3 to ensure that the coefficient of the x's has same absolute value of 3 in both equations. (i.e. a value of 3 regardless of the sign).

N.B. If we had chosen to make the coefficients of y the same in both equations we would have multiplied (i) by 3 and (ii) by 2, thus making the coefficient of y in both equations equal to 6.

Multiplying (ii) by 3 we obtain

$$-3x + 2y = 1 .... \text{(i)}$$
$$3x + 9y = 54 .... \text{(ii) multiplied by 3}$$

We can now eliminate the terms in x by adding these equations.

N.B. Because the sign of the coefficient of x is different in each of the two equations, subtracting the equations would not have eliminated the terms in x.

We now obtain

$$(-3x + 3x) + (2y + 9y) = 1 + 54$$
$$11y = 55$$
$$\mathbf{y = 5}$$

Substituting this value of y into one of our original equations, say (i), we obtain

$$-3x + 2y = 1$$
$$-3x + 2(5) = 1$$
$$-3x + 10 = 1$$
$$-3x = 1 - 10 = -9$$
$$\mathbf{x = 3}$$

Hence our solution is

$$x = 3, \quad y = 5$$

We could now verify that this solution is correct by substituting it back into equations (i) and (ii).

EXAMPLE 4

Solve $\dfrac{4x - 3}{y} = 3$

$\dfrac{6y}{7x} = 1$

The first step is to express the equations to be solved in a simpler form. If we consider the first equation we have:

$$\frac{4x - 3}{y} = 3$$

Multiplying both sides of this equation by y, we have

$4x - 3 = 3y$

Which, after rearranging, becomes

$4x - 3y = 3$ ...... (i)

If we now consider the second of the original equations, we have:

$\dfrac{6y}{7x} = 1$

Multiplying both sides of this equation by 7x, we have

$6y = 7x$

which, after rearranging, becomes

$7x - 6y = 0$ ...... (ii)

Hence the two equations to be solved can now be written as follows:

$4x - 3y = 3$ ...... (i)
$7x - 6y = 0$ ...... (ii)

If we now multiply equation (i) by 2 then we will be in a position to eliminate the terms in y. We thus have:

$8x - 6y = 6$ ...... (i) multiplied by 2
$7x - 6y = 0$ ...... (ii)

We can now eliminate the terms in y by subtracting these equations. We hence obtain:

$$(8x - 6y) - (7x - 6y) = 6 - 0$$
$$8x - 6y - 7x + 6y = 6$$
$$x = 6$$

Substituting this value of x into one of the original equations, say

$$\frac{6y}{7x} = 1$$

we have

$$\frac{6y}{7(6)} = 1$$
$$6y = 42$$
$$y = 7$$

Hence our solution is

$$x = 6 \qquad y = 7$$

GENERAL EXERCISES

EXERCISE 1   Solve the following by elimination:

i) $\begin{aligned} x + y &= 5 \\ x + 4y &= 14 \end{aligned}$

ii) $\begin{aligned} 2x + 3y &= -1 \\ 2x - y &= 3 \end{aligned}$

iii) $\begin{aligned} 3x - y &= 7 \\ 2x + y &= 13 \end{aligned}$

EXERCISE 2   Solve the following by substitution:

i) $\begin{aligned} x + 7y &= 16 \\ 2x + 3y &= 10 \end{aligned}$

ii) $\begin{aligned} 4x - y &= -14 \\ 3x + 5y &= 1 \end{aligned}$

EXERCISE 3   Solve the following graphically:

i) $\begin{aligned} x - y &= 3 \\ 6x + 3y &= 27 \end{aligned}$

ii) $\begin{aligned} 2x + 3y &= 19 \\ 3x - 2y &= -4 \end{aligned}$

EXERCISE 4   Solve the following first by elimination, then by substitution, and then graphically:

i) $\begin{aligned} 3x - 4y &= -27 \\ 2x + 5y &= 28 \end{aligned}$

ii) $\begin{aligned} -3x + 2y &= 5 \\ 4x + 3y &= -18 \end{aligned}$

EXERCISE 5   Solve the following:

i) $\begin{aligned} 2x - 3y &= 10 \\ x + 5y &= -14\tfrac{1}{2} \end{aligned}$

ii) $\quad y - x \quad = -2\,\tfrac{3}{4}$
$\quad\quad 2x + 4y \ = \ 7$

iii) $\quad x + 7 \quad = \ y$
$\quad\quad 3x + 2y \ = -11$

iv) $\quad 5a + 3b \ = 3$
$\quad\quad 4a - 2b \ = 9$

v) $\quad \dfrac{2x}{3} + y \ = \ \dfrac{11}{30}$

$\quad\quad x - \dfrac{y}{4} = \dfrac{1}{5}$

vi) $\quad \dfrac{3x}{y} = 5$

$\quad\quad 4x - y = -1\,^{13}/_{21}$

vii) $\quad \dfrac{p + 4}{q} = 2$

$\quad\quad \dfrac{5p - 1}{3q} = 1$

viii) $\quad \dfrac{-222x - 6}{4y} = -3$

$\quad\quad \dfrac{y - 7}{x + 5} \ = 2$

UNIT 9 – SIMULTANEOUS EQUATIONS
SOLUTIONS TO EXERCISES

1. i) $x = 2,$ $y = 3$
    ii) $x = 1,$ $y = -1$
    iii) $x = 4,$ $y = 5$

2. i) $x = 2,$ $y = 2$
    ii) $x = -3,$ $y = 2$

3. i) $x = 4,$ $y = 1$
    ii) $x = 2,$ $y = 5$

4. i) $x = -1,$ $y = 6$
    ii) $x = -3,$ $y = -2$

5. i) $x = \tfrac{1}{2},$ $y = -3$
    ii) $x = 3,$ $y = \tfrac{1}{4}$
    iii) $x = -5,$ $y = 2$
    iv) $a = 1\tfrac{1}{2},$ $b = -1\tfrac{1}{2}$
    v) $x = \tfrac{1}{4},$ $y = \tfrac{1}{5}$
    vi) $x = -^{10}/_{21},$ $y = -^{2}/_{7}$
    vii) $p = 2,$ $q = 3$
    viii) $x = 1,$ $y = 19$

10. QUADRATIC EQUATIONS

INTRODUCTION

A quadratic function is a function of the form

$$y = ax^2 + bx + c \quad \ldots\ldots\ldots\ldots\ldots (1)$$

where a, b, c are constants, and $a \neq 0$

Examples of the graphs of quadratic functions are given below:

Fig 1

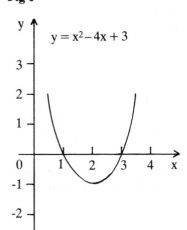

$y = x^2 - 4x + 3$

Fig 2

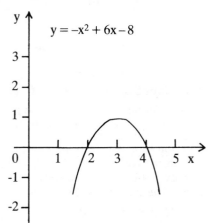

$y = -x^2 + 6x - 8$

A quadratic equation may be written in the form

$$ax^2 + bx + c = 0 \quad \ldots\ldots\ldots\ldots\ldots (2)$$

where a, b, c are constants, and $a \neq 0$

Note that this corresponds to putting y = 0 in the quadratic function (1)

The solution of the quadratic equation (2) is given by

$$x = \frac{-b \pm \sqrt{b^2 - 4ac}}{2a} \quad \ldots\ldots\ldots\ldots\ldots\ldots (3)$$

N.B. The derivation of formula (3) is not considered here.

It should be noted that if $b^2 - 4ac < 0$ then (3) involves taking the square root of a negative number. This is not possible in terms of real numbers and such cases are not considered here.

EXAMPLE 1

Solve $x^2 - 4x + 3 = 0$

Comparing this equation with (2) we see that

$a = 1;$ $b = -4;$ $c = 3$

(a is the coefficient of x^2; b is the coefficient of x; and c is the constant term)

Using (3) we obtain

$$x = \frac{-b \pm \sqrt{b^2 - 4ac}}{2a} = \frac{4 \pm \sqrt{(-4)^2 - 4(1)(3)}}{2(1)}$$

$$x = \frac{4 \pm \sqrt{16 - 12}}{2} = \frac{4 \pm \sqrt{4}}{2}$$

$$x = \frac{4 \pm 2}{2} = \frac{6}{2} \text{ and } \frac{2}{2}$$

i.e. $x = 3, 1$

The solution of $x^2 - 4x + 3 = 0$ is $x = 1$ and $x = 3$

This can be verified by looking at Fig 1 (i.e. the solution occurs where the curve $y = x^2 - 4x + 3$ cuts the x axis).

Solution by Factorisation

An alternative method of solving a quadratic equation is factorisation. However, this method is only easily applied to some quadratic equations. The method is illustrated as follows:

$$x^2 - 4x + 3 = 0$$

To factorise the left hand side of this equation we require two numbers the sum of which is -4 (the coefficient of x) and the product of which is 3 (the constant term). These numbers are -3 and -1, and the factors are $(x - 3)$ and $(x - 1)$. We now have:

$$x^2 - 4x + 3 = 0$$
$$(x - 3)(x - 1) = 0$$

The two terms $(x - 3)$ and $(x - 1)$ have a product of zero if either one of the terms equals zero. Therefore the solution of our quadratic equation is

$(x - 3) = 0$ or $(x - 1) = 0$
$x = 3$ or $x = 1$

EXAMPLE 2

Solve $-x^2 + 6x - 8 = 0$

Comparing this equation with (2), we have

$a = -1;$ $b = 6;$ $c = -8$

Using (3) we obtain

$$x = \frac{-b \pm \sqrt{b^2 - 4ac}}{2a}$$

$$x = \frac{-6 \pm \sqrt{6^2 - 4(-1)(-8)}}{2(-1)} = \frac{-6 \pm \sqrt{36 - 32}}{-2}$$

$$x = \frac{-6 \pm \sqrt{4}}{-2} = \frac{-6 \pm 2}{-2} = \frac{-8}{-2} \text{ and } \frac{-4}{-2}$$

i.e.   **x = 4, 2**

This can be verified by looking at Fig. 2.

Alternatively, using the method of factorisation described in example 1, we have:

$$-x^2 + 6x - 8 = 0$$
$$x^2 - 6x + 8 = 0$$
$$(x - 4)(x - 2) = 0$$
$$x = 4, \ 2$$

EXAMPLE 3

Solve $4x^2 - 14x + 12 = 0$

The calculations can be made simpler here if the equation is first divided through (on both sides) by 2.

Hence we obtain

$2x^2 - 7x + 6 = 0$

In this case we have

$a = 2;$ $b = -7;$ $c = 6;$

and hence

$$x = \frac{-b \pm \sqrt{b^2 - 4ac}}{2a} = \frac{7 \pm \sqrt{49 - 4(2)(6)}}{2(2)} = \frac{7 \pm \sqrt{49 - 48}}{4}$$

$$x = \frac{7 \pm \sqrt{1}}{4} = \frac{7 \pm 1}{4} = \frac{8}{4}, \frac{6}{4}$$

x = 2, 1 ½

EXERCISES   Questions similar to examples 1,2 and 3.

Solve the following:

i) $x^2 - 5x + 4 = 0$
ii) $-2x^2 - 4x + 6 = 0$
iii) $x^2 - 3x = 10$

iv) $6x^2 = 1-x$
v) $x^2 -4x + 4 = 0$

EXAMPLE 4

Solve $3x^2 - 48 = 0$

Here we have

$a = 3;$ $b = 0;$ $c = -48$

and hence

$$x = \frac{-b \pm \sqrt{b^2-4ac}}{2a} = \frac{0 \pm \sqrt{0-4(3)(-48)}}{2(3)} = \frac{\pm \sqrt{576}}{6} = \frac{\pm 24}{6}$$

$x = \pm 4$

This example is a special case because $b = 0$. Whenever this case arises it is not necessary to employ the quadratic formula given by (3). Instead we could have treated this example as follows:

$3x^2 - 48 = 0$

Moving -48 to the R.H.S. of the equation (i.e. by adding 48 to both sides of the equation) we obtain

$3x^2 = 48$

dividing through by 3 we obtain

$$x^2 = {}^{48}/_3 = 16$$
$$x^2 = 16$$

Hence $x = \pm 4$

EXERCISES   Questions similar to example 4.

Solve the following:

i) $x^2 - 25 = 0$
ii) $x^2 = 49$
iii) $4x^2 - 576 = 0$
iv) $x^2 - 1 = 0$
v) $16x^2 - 1 = 0$

EXAMPLE 5

Solve $x^2 - 8x = 0$

Here we have

$a = 1;$ $b = -8;$ $c = 0$

Hence

$$x = \frac{-b \pm \sqrt{b^2-4ac}}{2a} = \frac{8 \pm \sqrt{(-8)^2-4(1)(0)}}{2(1)} = \frac{8 \pm \sqrt{64-0}}{2}$$

$$x = \frac{8 \pm \sqrt{64}}{2} = \frac{8 \pm 8}{2} = \frac{16}{2} , \ 0$$

$x = 0, 8$

This example is a special case because $c = 0$. Whenever this case arises it is not necessary to employ the quadratic formula given by (3). Instead we could have treated this example as follows:

$$x^2 - 8x = 0$$

Because both terms on the L.H.S. contain x, we can write this equation as

$$x(x - 8) = 0$$

That is $x = 0$ or $(x - 8) = 0$

Hence the solution is **$x = 0$ and 8**

EXERCISES   Questions similar to example 5.

Solve the following:

i) $x^2 - 6x = 0$
ii) $-3x^2 + 6x = 0$
iii) $4x^2 - 12x = 0$
iv) $3x^2 - x = 0$
v) $7x^2 = -x$

EXAMPLE 6

Solve

$$(x - 2)(x - 3) = 2x - 6$$

The first step is to expand the brackets and we have:

$$(x - 2)(x - 3) = 2x - 6$$
$$x^2 - 5x + 6 = 2x - 6$$

Rearranging this equation we have

$$x^2 - 7x + 12 = 0$$

We can now solve in the usual way. We have

$$a = 1; \qquad b = -7; \qquad c = 12;$$

and hence

$$x = \frac{-b \pm \sqrt{b^2 - 4ac}}{2a} = \frac{7 \pm \sqrt{49 - 48}}{2} = \frac{7 \pm 1}{2} = \frac{8}{2}, \frac{6}{2}$$

Hence the solution is

$x = 4, 3$

GENERAL EXERCISES

Solve the following:

i) $x^2 - 8x + 7 = 0$
ii) $3x^2 - 14x + 8 = 0$
iii) $-8x^2 - 6x - 1 = 0$

iv) $3x^2 - 300 = 0$
v) $10x^2 - x = 0$
vi) $42x^2 = 13x - 1$
vii) $(x - 8)(x - 4) + 3 = 0$
viii) $-2z^2 + 19z - 24 = 0$
ix) $y^2 - 10y + 25 = 0$
x) $-4x^2 = 3x$

UNIT 10 – QUADRATIC EQUATIONS
SOLUTIONS TO EXERCISES

1.   Questions similar to examples 1, 2 and 3.
   i) $x = 1, \ 4$
   ii) $x = -3, \ 1$
   iii) $x = -2, \ 5$
   iv) $x = -\frac{1}{2}, \ \frac{1}{3}$
   v) $x = 2$

2.   Questions similar to example 4.
   i) $x = \pm 5$
   ii) $x = \pm 7$
   iii) $x = \pm 12$
   vi) $x = \pm 1$
   v) $x = \pm \frac{1}{4}$

3.   Questions similar to example 5.
   i) $x = 0, \ 6$
   ii) $x = 0, \ 2$
   iii) $x = 0, \ 3$
   iv) $x = 0, \ \frac{1}{3}$
   v) $x = 0, \ -\frac{1}{7}$

4.   General Exercises
   i) $x = 1, \ 7$
   ii) $x = \frac{2}{3}, \ 4$
   iii) $x = -\frac{1}{2}, \ -\frac{1}{4}$
   iv) $x = \pm 10$
   v) $x = 0, \ \frac{1}{10}$
   vi) $x = \frac{1}{6}, \ \frac{1}{7}$
   vii) $x = 5, \ 7$
   viii) $z = 1\frac{1}{2}, \ 8$
   ix) $y = 5$
   x) $x = 0, \ -\frac{3}{4}$

ACHIEVEMENT TEST

This test should be completed within a reasonable time period (say two hours maximum) without the aid of the units.

Because the achievement test is intended to test your arithmetical skills (as well as your understanding of principles and concepts), ideally you should not use a calculator.

1. a) Express $^{10}/_{16}$ in its simplest form.
    b) Express $^{55}/_{25}$ in its simplest form.

2. Evaluate the following:
    a) $^{3}/_{7} \times ^{4}/_{9}$
    b) $3\frac{1}{2} + ^{7}/_{8} - ^{3}/_{16}$
    c) $(2\frac{1}{4} \div 2\frac{2}{5}) \times \frac{1}{3}$
    d) $\dfrac{(2 + ^{4}/_{5} - 1\frac{1}{3})}{1\frac{2}{3} - ^{5}/_{11}}$

3. a) Transform 5.021 into a fraction.
    b) Transform $4\,^{27}/_{32}$ into a decimal.

4. Evaluate the following:
    a) $0.32 + 7.15 - 2.16$
    b) $0.31 \div 2$
    c) 2.751×0.34
    d) $\dfrac{4.2(3.71 - 1.004)}{0.01 + 3.29}$

5. a) Express $^{5}/_{32}$ as a percentage.
    b) Express 0.5625 as a percentage.
    c) Express 39% as a decimal.
    d) Express 65% as a fraction.

6. a) Calculate 15% of 613.
    b) Calculate $8\frac{1}{4}\%$ of 33.
    c) Increase 119 by $12\,^{2}/_{5}\%$.
    d) Decrease 86 by 17%.

7. Evaluate the following for $x = 2$; $y = 3$; $z = -5$.
    a) $2x + y + z$
    b) $3x - y - 4z$
    c) $2x - z$
    d) $x + z$
    e) $\dfrac{2z}{5} + \dfrac{x}{2} + \dfrac{y}{3}$

8. Expand the following:
    a) $3(2x - 5y)$
    b) $(a + b)(a - b)$
    c) $5(x + y)(2x^2 - 3x - y)$

9. Evaluate the following:
    a) $(7^6 \times 7^3) \div 7^4$
    b) $625^{-1/4}$
    c) $\sqrt{(a^3)^6}$
    d) $(\frac{1}{8})^{-1/3}$
    e) $3^2 \times 27^{5/3}$

10. Draw a graph of the following functions for $-3 \leqslant x \leqslant 3$.
    a) $y = 7x + 3$
    b) $y = 2x^3 - 24x + 18$

11. Solve the following for x:
    a) $13x - 7 = 4x + 20$
    b) $\frac{1}{4}(-2 + 5x) = 7$
    c) $\dfrac{1}{(x-3)} = \dfrac{4}{x}$
    d) $-\frac{1}{2} + 4(3 - x) = 5(x - 2) - 1$

12. Solve the following pairs of simultaneous equations:
    a) $3x - y = -1$
    　　　$x + 4y = 17$
    b) $\dfrac{6x - 4y}{x + 3y} = 2$
    　　　$\dfrac{2x + 4}{y} = 7$

13. Solve the following equations for x:
    a) $x^2 - 3x = 0$
    b) $x^2 - 16 = 0$
    c) $x^2 - 11x + 18 = 0$
    d) $2x^2 - 5x + 2 = 0$

14. Find the equation of the straight line passing through the following pairs of points:
    a) $(0, \ 0)$ and $(1, \ 3)$
    b) $(-2, \ 1)$ and $(3, \ 2)$

ACHIEVEMENT TEST ANSWERS

1. a) $5/8$
   b) $2\,1/5$

2. a) $4/21$
   b) $4\,3/16$
   c) $5/16$
   d) $1\,21/100$

3. a) $5\,21/1000$
   b) 4.84375

4. a) 5.31
   b) 0.155
   c) 0.93534
   d) 3.444

5. a) 15.625%
   b) 56.25%
   c) 0.39
   d) $13/20$

6. a) 91.95
   b) 2.7225
   c) 133.756
   d) 71.38

7. a) 2
   b) 23
   c) 9
   d) -3
   e) 0

8. a) $6x - 15y$
   b) $a^2 - b^2$
   c) $10x^3 - 15x^2 + 10x^2y - 5y^2 - 20xy$

9. a) 7^5
   b) $1/5$
   c) a^9
   d) 2
   e) 3^7

10. a) $y = 7x + 3$

x:	-3	-2	-1	0	1	2	3
y:	-18	-11	-4	3	10	17	24

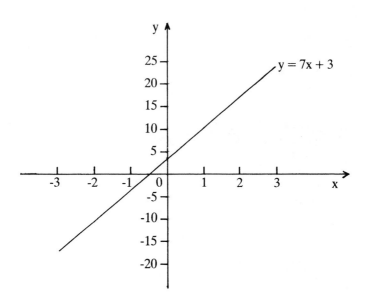

b) $y = 2x^3 - 24x + 18$

x:	-3	-2	-1	0	1	2	3
y:	36	50	40	18	-4	-14	0

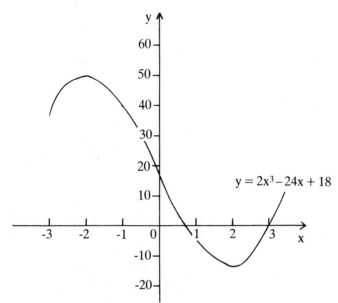

$y = 2x^3 - 24x + 18$

11. a) $x = 3$
    b) $x = 6$
    c) $x = 4$
    d) $x = 2\frac{1}{2}$

12. a) $x = 1; \ y = 4;$
    b) $x = 5; \ y = 2:$

13. a) $x = 0, 3$
    b) $x = \pm 4$
    c) $x = 2, \ 9$
    d) $x = 2, \ \frac{1}{2}$

14. a) $y = 3x$
    b) $y = \frac{1}{5}(x + 7)$

ACHIEVEMENT TEST
MARKING SCHEME

Question	Marks	Question	Marks
1a	1	8a	2
1b	1	8b	3
2a	1	8c	3
2b	1	9a	2
2c	2	9b	3
2d	3	9c	3
3a	1	9d	4
3b	2	9e	4
4a	1	10a	4
4b	1	10b	4
4c	2	11a	2
4d	3	11b	3
5a	1	11c	3
5b	1	11d	3
5c	1	12a	2
5d	1	12b	4
6a	2	13a	2
6b	2	13b	2
6c	3	13c	2
6d	3	13d	2
7a	1	14a	2
7b	1	14b	2
7c	1		
7d	1		
7e	2		

TOTAL MARKS = 100

Guide to Achievement Test Marks

The following can be used as a guide to your performance in the test, although commom sense should prevail in distinguishing between marks which fall near the beginning or the end of the ranges of marks listed. For example there is obviously little difference between a mark of, say, 74 (which is classed as only a fair mark) and 75 (which is classed as a good mark).

Marks (out of 100)	Comment
Under 50	This is a low mark and clearly indicates that you need to study the units again.

50 – Under 60	This mark is below the standard expected and indicates that further study of the units is still necessary, especially of those topics associated with the questions incorrectly answered in the test.
60 – Under 75	This mark is only fair and indicates deficiencies in some topics. You would benefit by further study of those topics associated with the questions incorrectly answered in the test.
75 – Under 90	This is a good mark indicating that you have a reasonably sound knowledge of the topics covered. It would still benefit you to review those problems answered incorrectly in the test.
90 – 100	A very good mark. Well done!

TUTOR'S SECTION

This section is intended for use by tutors for homework or assessment purposes. It includes extra exercises on each of the ten units, and an extra achievement test, without worked solutions or answers.

Unit 1

Evaluate the following:

i) $\frac{3}{7} + \frac{1}{2}$

ii) $1\frac{1}{3} + 2\frac{3}{10}$

iii) $4\frac{2}{3} - 1\frac{1}{7} + 2\frac{1}{2}$

iv) $1\frac{4}{7} \times 2\frac{1}{3}$

v) $\frac{3}{4} \times 1\frac{1}{5} \times \frac{3}{8}$

vi) $7\frac{3}{8} \div \frac{4}{9}$

vii) $(\frac{1}{9} + \frac{3}{7}) \times 3\frac{1}{2}$

viii) $(1\frac{3}{4} - \frac{5}{12}) \div 2\frac{7}{8}$

ix) $(3\frac{1}{2} \times 2\frac{2}{3}) - (\frac{3}{10} \div \frac{2}{3})$

x) $\dfrac{(2\frac{1}{2} - 1\frac{1}{7} + \frac{9}{10})}{(1\frac{2}{3} \times \frac{3}{8})}$

Unit 2

Evaluate the following:

i) $0.32 + 3.27$

ii) $4.271 - 1.08$

iii) $0.003 + 12.0147$

iv) $9.2612 + 1.07 - 5.41$

v) 1.21×3.7

vi) $1.03 \times 2.1 \times 0.07$

vii) $86.273 \div 1.8$

viii) $126.404 \div 0.0012$

ix) $(18.006 \times 0.034) \div 0.13$

x) $\dfrac{(2.3 + 7.005)}{7.003 \times 1.2}$

Unit 3

i) Express $58\frac{1}{2}\%$ as a fraction

ii) Express $63\frac{7}{10}\%$ as a decimal

iii) Express $\frac{19}{20}$ as a percentage

iv) Express 0.093 as a percentage

v) Calculate 13% of 549

vi) Calculate $79\frac{3}{8}\%$ of 750

90

vii) Increase 89 by 8%
viii) Increase 126 by 17 ¾%
ix) Decrease 743 by 45%
x) Decrease 181 by 19 ³⁄₁₀%

Unit 4

Simplify the following (by combining like terms)

i) $3x + 2y + 4x^2 - 6x + 8y + 2xy$

ii) $\dfrac{3a}{4} - \dfrac{b}{5} + a^2 + \dfrac{a}{8} - \dfrac{b}{15} + \dfrac{a^2}{10}$

Factorise the following

iii) $a^4 b^3 c^2 + a^2 b^3 c^2 + a^3 b^2 c$

iv) $xy^2 - x^2y^2 + x^3 y^3 z^2$

v) $\dfrac{s^2t^2}{p} + \dfrac{st^3}{p^2} + \dfrac{st^2}{p^3}$

Expand the following

vi) $(2x - 1)(x + 7)$

vii) $(a^2 + b)(a^3 - b^2)$

viii) $7(p + q)(p - q - 5)$

ix) $4(a + b - c)(a - b - c)$

x) $\dfrac{y}{x}\left(\dfrac{2x}{3} + \dfrac{4}{y}\right)^2$

Unit 5

Evaluate the following:

i) $125^{-2/3}$

ii) $(\%_{16})^{-3/2}$

iii) $32^{3/5} \times 128^{2/7}$

iv) $\left[(^{27}\!/_{64})^{3/2} \div (^{27}\!/_{64})^{1/2} \right]^{1/3}$

Simplify the following:

v) $7ab \times a^3 b^4 \times 2a^2 b^2$

vi) $(x^2 y^2 \times x^3y) \div x^4y$

vii) $(x^{-3})^2 \div (xy)^{-4}$

viii) $(\sqrt{a^{-9}})^{-1}$

ix) $(b^{-3})^2 \times (\sqrt[4]{b^6})^{-1/2}$

x) $\dfrac{(x^3)^2 \times x^{-4}}{(\sqrt[4]{x^6})(x^2)}$

Unit 6

Draw graphs of the following functions for $-5 \leqslant x \leqslant 5$

i) $\quad y = x^2 - 2$
ii) $\quad y = x(x + 4)$
iii) $\quad y = 4x^2 - 13x + 3$
iv) $\quad y = x^3 - x^2 - 9x + 9$
v) $\quad y = \dfrac{20x}{x^2 + 1}$

Unit 7

Draw the graph of the following straight lines indicating where they cross the axes.

i) $\quad y = 12x$
ii) $\quad y = 7x + 3$
iii) $\quad y = 4 - 9x$
iv) $\quad y = \dfrac{9x + 16}{5}$

Calculate the equation of the straight line passing through the following points.

v) $\quad$ (2, 5) and (4, 8)
vi) $\quad$ (0, 0) and $(-3, -2)$
vii) $\quad$ (3, -1) and $(-3, 5)$
viii) $\quad$ (12, 18) and $(-3, 0)$
ix) $\quad$ (1, 2) and $(-5, -16)$
x) $\quad$ (1 ½, 3¼) and $(-2 \frac{1}{8}, -3 \frac{1}{5})$

Unit 8

Solve the following:

i) $\quad 4x - 1 = 7x + 5$
ii) $\quad 2(3x - 7) = 4$
iii) $\quad 2(x + 9) = 7x - 2$
iv) $\quad \dfrac{4x}{9} = \dfrac{28}{5}$
v) $\quad 2x - 3 = \frac{1}{5}(x + 7) - 2$
vi) $\quad \frac{x}{5} + 2 = 1 - 3x$
vii) $\quad \frac{3}{4}(x + 5) = \frac{2}{5}(x + 4)$
viii) $\quad \dfrac{4}{7-x} = 2$
ix) $\quad \dfrac{2}{x} = \dfrac{9}{x+3}$
x) $\quad 3\left[\dfrac{5x - 4}{8}\right] = \dfrac{x}{2} + 3 - 2(x - 1)$

Unit 9
Solve the following:

i) $x + y = 5$
     $x + 7y = 17$

ii) $2x + y = 19$
     $4x - y = 35$

iii) $4x - 5y = -11$
     $3x + 2y = 32$

iv) $7x - y = 22$
     $x - 3y = 6$

v) $3x = 10y$
     $x + y = 6\frac{1}{2}$

vi) $2(x + 1) + y = -4$
     $3(x + y) = -15$

vii) $2x + \frac{y}{4} = 1\frac{1}{16}$

     $\frac{x}{3} - \frac{y}{2} = \frac{1}{24}$

viii) $\frac{8x}{y} = -4$

     $3x - 5 = -5\frac{3}{10}$

ix) $\frac{4x - 1}{y} = \frac{1}{2}$

     $\frac{3x - 2}{3y} = \frac{1}{18}$

x) $\frac{x + 3}{y + 2} = \frac{48}{17}$

     $\frac{2y - 7}{x - 1} = \frac{-27}{8}$

Unit 10
Solve the following

i) $x^2 - 3x + 2 = 0$
ii) $x^2 - 14x + 45 = 0$
iii) $4x^2 = 64$
iv) $9x^2 - 81 = 0$
v) $3x^2 - 42x = 0$
vi) $5x^2 = x$
vii) $(x - 4)(x - 7) = 2x - 12$
viii) $6x^2 - 17x = -5$
ix) $-32x^2 + 52x - 15 = 0$
x) $\frac{x(x - 13)}{12} = -3$

Achievement Test

The duration of this test, and whether or not a calculator may be used, will be decided by the tutor.

1. Express $^{84}/_{14}$ in its simplest form.

2. a) Express 0.0037 as a fraction
   b) Express $^{9}/_{16}$ as a decimal

3. Evaluate the following:
   a) $^{5}/_{8} + ^{2}/_{5}$
   b) $7\,^{9}/_{16} + ^{3}/_{8} - 4\,^{3}/_{10}$
   c) $4\,^{1}/_{2} \times 2\,^{5}/_{16}$
   d) $12\,^{7}/_{20} \div 5\,^{3}/_{5}$
   e) $\dfrac{1\,^{1}/_{8} \times 3\,^{3}/_{4}}{2\,^{3}/_{4}}$

4. Evaluate the following:
   a) $0.003 + 12.1 - 7.32$
   b) $0.638 \div 5$
   c) 0.7132×0.035
   d) $\dfrac{0.639 + 2.035}{4.7 - 3.1}$

5. a) Express $^{6}/_{25}$ as a percentage
   b) Express 0.7139 as a percentage
   c) Express 0.001 as a percentage
   d) Express 2% as a fraction
   e) Express 3% as a decimal

6. a) Calculate $12\,^{3}/_{4}\%$ of 1348
   b) Increase 738 by 8%
   c) Decrease 921 by $12\,^{1}/_{2}\%$

7. Simplify the following:
   a) $17x + 4y - 3x - 3y$
   b) $\dfrac{7x}{10} + 3x + \dfrac{x}{25}$

8. Evaluate the following for $x = 3$, $y = -2$, $z = ^{1}/_{2}$
   a) $x + 3y + z$
   b) $\dfrac{x}{3} - y - 5z$
   c) $z\,(x - y)$

9. Expand the following:
   a) $7(x - 4y + z)$
   b) $(x - y) (x^2 - 7x + y)$
   c) $-3(x - 2y)^2$
   d) $6(x + 2y) (x^2 - y)$

10. Evaluate the following:
    a) 2^{-3}
    b) $49^{-1/2} \times (1/4)^{-3}$
    c) $512^{1/3} \div 36^{3/2}$

11. Simplify the following:
    a) $(\sqrt[4]{x} \,)^5$
    b) $x^5 y^{-3} \div x^2 y$
    c) $\dfrac{(a^{-3}) (1/a)^{1/2}}{a^{4/3}}$

12. Draw a graph of the following for $-4 \leqslant x \leqslant 4$
    a) $y = 2x - 3$
    b) $y = 3x^2 - 3x - 6$

13. Find the equation of the straight line passing through the following pairs of points
    a) $(0, 0)$ and $(7, 2)$
    b) $(-3, 1)$ and $(4, 9)$

14. Solve the following for x
    a) $3x + 925 = 7x - 3$
    b) $\dfrac{7}{x - 5} = \dfrac{5}{2(x + 3)}$

15. Solve the following pairs of simultaneous equations
    a) $4x + y = 28$
       $3x - 2y = -1$
    b) $\dfrac{2x + 1}{y + 5} = \dfrac{-1}{9}$
       $\dfrac{x}{y + 3} = \dfrac{-1}{7}$

16. Solve the following for x
    a) $4x^2 - 401x + 100 = 0$
    b) $x(x - 15) = 30 - 4x$
    c) $\dfrac{2x (x - 50)}{3} = -150$

APPENDIX 1

A Note on Calculators

Calculators are an essential tool for any student on a course with a 'quantitative component'. If you are considering purchasing a calculator your choice will very much depend on your intended use of the calculator (i.e. the type of calculations you intend to perform and hence the function keys you require) and the price you are willing to pay. If you are a student it would be advisable to consult your course tutor before purchase.

Programmable calculators are generally more expensive and may well prove very helpful in your studies. However, if you intend to sit examinations that require you to show all your working they may only be of limited use. Again, you should consult your course tutor.

As far as the topics in this book are concerned readers are advised to use a calculator (not programmable) with the following facilities:

i)   The four basic functions $(+, -, \times, \div)$
ii) At least one memory store. More than one memory store is desirable, as are M+ and M− facilities.
iii) x^y and preferably $x^{1/y}$ keys to calculate powers and roots.

In addition you should ensure that the keypad of your calculator is comfortable to use (eg the keys are not too small for your fingers) as this will reduce the likelihood of accidentally touching the wrong key.

Using your Calculator

When using your calculator it is useful to remember the adage 'If all else fails, read the instructions'!

It is important to understand the calculation you are performing. Further, you should be able to identify an answer that is obviously wrong. If, for example, you attempt to divide 25 by 0.2 and get an answer of 5 (instead of correct answer of 125) then you should be able to recognise that this answer is obviously wrong – in this case you probably pressed the 'multiply' key instead of the 'divide' key.

Remember, a calculator is not a substitute for thinking, it is a tool that you control. It should not 'control' your calculations i.e. mistakes can be made when using a calculator and it is advisable to check your calculations.

EXAMPLE 1

Multiple calculations using the four basic functions (+ , − , × , ÷)

Most calculators will allow you to perform 'multiple' calculations without the need to press the equals (=) key between every step.

This is illustrated in the following example:

Evaluate using a calculator:
(From: Unit 2, Exercise (i), following Example 4)

$$0.47 + 3.846 + 2.00360$$

		Display Shows
STEP 1	enter 0.47 into the calculator	0.47
STEP 2	press the plus (+) key	
STEP 3	now enter 3.846	3.846
STEP 4	press the plus (+) key again	4.316

(N.B. you do not need to press the equals (=) key as the plus (+) key serves this purpose **and** sets the calculator up ready to receive another number)

STEP 5	now enter 2.00360	2.00360
STEP 6	press the equals (=) key	6.3196

MEMORY KEYS

Many calculators have a memory function that allows you to store results during a lengthy calculation to re-use later.

(N.B. Many also keep the value in memory even if the calculator is turned off (unless the batteries are also taken out), so be careful not to assume that the memory is automatically cleared when you turn off the calculator).

The most common menu keys are:

Memory in (Min) – this puts the value on the display into memory and **replaces** any previous value held in memory.

Memory add (M+) – this puts the value on the display into memory and **adds** it to any previous value held in memory

(Some calculators also have a Memory subtract (M−) key that subtracts from the value stored in memory rather than adding to it).

Memory recall (MR) – this recalls the value from memory, but it does not necessarily clear the memory. Some calculators still retain the value in memory even after a Memory recall.

Please Note: Even though calculators have a memory function, you will still need to tackle any question in the correct order. For example, you should attempt to avoid being in the situation where you need to store **two** numbers at the same time – which is impossible with only one memory – so when solving a fraction you should start with the denominator.

EXAMPLE 2

Using memory to save intermediate results

Evaluate:

(From: Unit 1, General Exercises (xxii) expressed in decimal format)

$$\frac{(8.25 \times 1.5)}{(4.5 + 4.25)}$$

		Display Shows
STEP 1	enter 4.5 into the calculator	4.5
STEP 2	press the plus (+) key	
STEP 3	enter 4.25	4.25
STEP 4	press the equals (=) key	8.75
STEP 5	press the memory in (Min) key	

(this puts the 8.75 into memory and allows us to start on the numerator)

STEP 6	enter 8.25	8.25
STEP 7	press the multiply (×) key	
STEP 8	enter 1.5	1.5
STEP 9	press the equals (=) key	12.375
STEP 10	press the divide (÷) key	
STEP 11	press the memory recall (MR) key	8.75

(this recalls the value of the denominator we placed into memory)

STEP 12	press the equals (=) key	1.4142857

which we can round *(Using three decimal places)* to 1.414

POWERS

The powers (x^y) key is vital to many calculations. Some calculators also have negative power (x^{-y}) and fractional power $(x^{1/y})$ keys. These are useful but not essential, as illustrated in the following examples:

EXAMPLE 3
Raising to a Power
    Evaluate 3^5

		Display Shows
STEP 1	enter 3 into the calculator	3
STEP 2	press the powers (x^y) key	
STEP 3	enter 5	5
STEP 4	press the equals (=) key	243

EXAMPLE 4
Raising to a Negative Power
    Evaluate 3^{-5}

		Display Shows
STEP 1	enter 3 into the calculator	3
STEP 2	press the powers (x^y) key	
STEP 3	enter 5	5
STEP 4	press the sign change ($^+/_-$) key	-5

(this is so we can raise to the power of a negative number)

STEP 5	press the equals (=) key	$4.1152263^{-0.3}$

i.e. 0.004115 *(when rounded to 6 decimal places)*

EXAMPLE 5
Raising to a Fractional Power
    Evaluate $3^{1/5}$

		Display Shows
STEP 1	enter 1 into the calculator	1
STEP 2	press the plus ($\div$) key	
STEP 3	enter 5	5
STEP 4	press the equals (=) key	0.2
STEP 5	press the memory in (Min) key	
STEP 6	enter 3	3
STEP 7	press the powers (x^y) key	
STEP 8	press the memory recall (MR) key	0.2

(recalls the 0.2, so we can raise to the power of a fraction)

STEP 9	press the equals (=) key	1.2457309

which we can round *(using three decimal places)* to 1.246

Using a calculator where the 'powers' (x^y) key is provided as a second function.

Some calculators do not have a separate key from 'powers', but add this operation to another key as a 'second' function. This is noted by placing the powers symbol (x^y) just above the key, often in a different colour. To use the function you must **first** press a 'function' key (marked Func, INV, 2nd, or Shift) and then the 'powers' key.

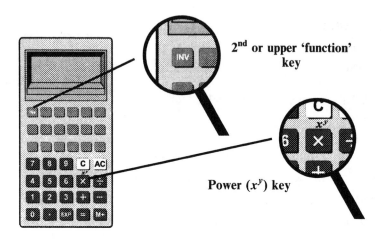

2nd or upper 'function' key

Power (x^y) key

COMMON DIFFICULTIES AND THEIR RESOLUTION

EXAMPLE 6

Multiple calculations involving products in the denominator

Evaluate:

(From: Unit 1, General Exercises (xxiii) expressed in decimal format)

$$\frac{(3 + 1.75 - 2.33)}{(0.4 \times 1.75)}$$

The easiest way to evaluate this problem using a calculator is to solve the denominator (0.4×1.75) first, put the result into memory and then recall and divide by it after having solved the numerator; as shown below:

		Display Shows
STEP 1	enter 0.4 into the calculator	0.4
STEP 2	press the (×) key	
STEP 3	enter 1.75	1.75
STEP 4	press the equals (=) key	0.7
STEP 5	press the (Min) key	
STEP 6	enter 3	3
STEP 7	press the plus (+) key	
STEP 8	enter 1.75	1.75
STEP 9	press the minus (−) key	4.75
STEP 10	enter 2.33	2.33
STEP 11	press the (=) key	2.42
STEP 12	press the divide (÷) key	
STEP 13	press the memory recall (MR) key	0.7
STEP 14	press the equals (=) key	3.4571429

which can be rounded *(using three decimal places)* to 3.457

However, assuming that you start the calculation by evaluating the numerator first, be careful of the following error:

		Display Shows
STEP 1	enter 3 into the calculator	3
STEP 2	press the plus (+) key	
STEP 3	enter 1.75	1.75
STEP 4	press the minus (−) key	4.75
STEP 5	enter 2.33	2.33
STEP 6	press the equals (=) key	2.42
STEP 7	press the plus (÷) key	

STEP 8   enter 0.4   0.4
STEP 9   press the divide (÷) key again   6.05

*(This is where the common error occurs – many people see the multiplication sign (×) in the denominator and press this key for step 9. It is an easy error to make, but the division by 0..4 has **already** taken place. What we now need to do is divide by 1.75 so we need the divide (÷) key. Of course we could not have performed this multiple division if the denominator had been (0.4 + 1.75); we would have needed to add the 0.4 and 1.75 together first.)*

Display Shows

STEP 10   enter 1.75   1.75
STEP 11   press the equals (=) key   3.4571429

which can be rounded *(using three decimal places)* to 3.457

(N.B. In Step 6 we needed to press the equals (=) key in order to complete the subtraction. Many calculators will not use either the multiply (×) or the divide (÷) keys to complete a calculation, so you should check the instructions. For example:

$$\frac{2+3}{5} \text{ requires entering as } 2(+)3(=)5(÷)5(=)1$$

the 'extra' (=) key being required before the division, otherwise the following will occur:

$$2 + \tfrac{3}{5} = 2.6$$

So be careful with multiple calculations. If in doubt, it does no harm to press the equals (=) key between each step.)

EXAMPLE 7

Using $\dfrac{1}{x}$ to divide by multiplying

Although it is always advisable to start multiple calculations with the denominator, the following illustrates an alternative technique. It also overcomes the problem of trying to store two numbers in the calculator memory at the same time. Here we use the earlier Example 2, but this time starting with the numerator instead of the denominator.

Evaluate:
(From: Unit 1, General Exercises (xxii) expressed in decimal format)

$$\frac{(8.25 \times 1.5)}{(4.5 + 4.25)}$$

		Display Shows
STEP 1	enter 8.25 into the calculator	8.25
STEP 2	press the multiply (×) key	
STEP 3	enter 1.5	1.5
STEP 4	press the equals (=) key	12.375
STEP 5	press the memory in (Min) key	
STEP 6	enter 4.5	4.5
STEP 7	press the plus (+) key	
STEP 8	enter 4.25	4.25
STEP 9	press the equals (=) key	8.75

*(Now we hit the problem – we want to divide by this number, but we cannot put it into memory without losing the 12.375 already stored there... So the solution to this problem is to **invert** the 8.75 and **multiply** by the result.*

(If you have an 'invert' function key (1/x) you should use this instead of Steps 10–12, but otherwise you can use the (x^y) key as shown overleaf)

		Display Shows
STEP 10	press the powers (x^y) key	
STEP 11	enter 1	1
STEP 12	press the sign change $^+/_-$	−1
STEP 13	press the equals (=) key	0.1142857

*(Note how raising a number, x, to the power of −1 (i.e. using (x^y) where y = −1) is the **same** as inverting the number i.e. (1/x)*

STEP 14	press the multiply (×) key	
STEP 15	press the memory recall (MR) key	12.375
STEP 16	press the equals (=) key	1.4142857

or *(rounding to 3 decimal places)* 1.414 as before.

APPENDIX 2

Rounding

When performing arithmetic calculations it is often necessary to 'round off a number' to a certain number of decimal places i.e. only a certain number of digits after the decimal point are retained and the remainder discarded. For example, if you were performing a financial calculation involving pounds and pence, and you obtained an answer of £2157.570163..., you would probably decide that it is not necessary to retain more than two digits after the decimal point. Two questions immediately arise:

–   How do you express a number correct to a certain number of decimal places i.e. how do you round off a number?

–   When performing arithmetic calculations, how many decimal places should be retained during your calculations?

1)   To apply the usual method for rounding off a number to a certain number of decimal places, say n decimal places, we must first examine the digit immediately after the nth decimal place. If this digit is 5 or more we round up the digit in the nth place (i.e. we increase it by 1) and discard the remaining digits to the right. If the digit immediately after the nth decimal place is less then 5 then the digit in the nth place remains unchanged and the remaining digits to the right are discarded.

For example, consider the number

12.76382

If we round off this number to a given number of decimal places then we obtain:

12.7638   (to 4 decimal places)
12.764   (to 3 decimal places)
12.76   (to 2 decimal places)
12.8   (to 1 decimal place)

As another example consider:

$\pi = 3.14159265...$

If we round this number off then we obtain:

3.14   (to 2 decimal places)
3.142   (to 3 decimal places)
3.1416   (to 4 decimal places)
3.14159   (to 5 decimal places)

2)   There is no one correct answer to the general question 'How many decimal places should I round to?' It is important to have

an understanding of the subsequent implications of discarding some digits (i.e. rounding) and much depends upon the situation. Rounding numbers in the intermediate stages of a calculation is risky and should be carried out with care. 'Rounding' invariably involves a loss of accuracy which can be compounded over a series of calculations to introduce a very serious error. When you are performing a calculation (involving several stages) you should, as a general rule, retain as many decimal places/ digits as it practicable during the intermediate stages of the calculation. At the end of the calculation you can then round off to the required number of decimal places. At all stages during the calculation you should retain, at the very least, one more decimal place than you require in your final answer i.e. If you are rounding each stage of your calculation to 3 decimal places, say, you cannot expect your final answer to be accurate to 3 (or more) decimal places.

Also available in the series: